Santorini

Guide to
Santorini

John Bowman

EFSTATHIADIS
GROUP

ISBN 960 226 191 9

Photograph by J. Bowman & M. Granitsas.

New Impression 1993

Printed and bound in Greece by
EΓSTATHIADIS GROUP S.A.

Distributed by
EFSTATHIADIS GROUP S.A.
HEAD OFFICE: AGIOU ATHANASIOU ST. GR - 145 65 ANIXI ATTIKIS
TEL: (01) 8140602, 8140702 FAX: (01) 8142915 TELEX: 216176 EF
ATHENS BRANCH: 14 VALTETSIOU ST. GR - 106 80 ATHENS
TEL: (01) 3633319, 3614312, 3637284 FAX: (01) 3614312
ATHENS BOOKSHOP: 84 ACADEMIAS ST. TEL: 3637439
THESSALONIKI BRANCH: 4 C. CRISTALLI ST. ANTIGONIDON SQUARE
THESSALONIKI, GR - 546 30 TEL: (031) 511781, 542498, FAX 544759
THESSALONIKI BOOKSHOP: 14 ETHNIKIS AMINIS ST. TEL: (031) 278158.

CONTENTS

HINTS TO USERS OF THIS GUIDE

1. Many of the details of tourism inevitably change from year to year: transportation fares, hotel prices, admission fees, and prices of all kinds increase; opening hours of museums and other facilities vary; ship and bus schedules change; etc. This guide gives the best available data, but rather than claiming to give the correct specifics in every case, we explain the general situation and any particular problems to be aware of. And beyond preparing everyone for such changes, we say to anyone who expects to be affected by particulars (such as a bus or boat schedule, entry hours, etc.) to inquire immediately upon arriving on Santorini. (See section on Information and Assistance: p. 86).

2. Streets and places in Fira may be located on the town plan on the inside of the back cover by using the grid system; they are so indicated throughout the book.

3. A discussion of the ways to make best use of a limited time on Santorini is on pages 72-75).

4. Note that the account (pp. 111-127) of the exhibition of the remains from the new Minoan-era site at Akrotiri had to go to press before the new museum in Fira opened; these and other objects may in fact still be on exhibit at the National Archaeological Museum in Athens. Inquire.

5. If anyone needs reminding, Santorini can be extremely photogenic; but it is also a place that rewards anyone with binoculars.

6. In place of an Index, there is a detailed Table of Contents in the front: this should allow people to locate anything.

View of Fira and Skaros (in the background).

A view of the island's capital.

The island of Nea Kameni (Volcano) as seen from Thera.

INTRODUCTION

A Special Island

Of the many Greek islands that attract visitors, perhaps none is more extraordinary than Santorini. Other islands may support more glamorous touristic developements, more ambitious archaeological remains, more textured historical associations, more varied landscapes. But none combines such an intense interaction between a natural terrain and human efforts. Over the millenniums, this interaction has produced some dramatic results — with at times nature having the upper hand, at times human beings. At the moment, humans seem to be "riding high", whether it is the native — literally perched on the edge of a volcano — or the visitors who buzz around the roads on motorbikes. This book is devoted to respecting all the various elements and individuals that cross paths on Santorini -- and to helping them all share the small spot of land with mutual respect. In subsequent pages, all the necessary ingredients for enjoying Santorini are detailed, but first we might consider a few general premises.

For most casual visitors to Santorini, the island and its way of life will be merely another chapter in the larger volume that is Greece. And to be sure, Santorini is much like other parts of Greece in its most obvious aspects. Although the Santorinians' language contains some localisms -- especially those from its Italian phase -- they speak Greek. Although there happens to be a Roman Catholic "presence", the Greek Orthodox religion predominates. Although there are some special foods, dances, and local traditions, the basic customs and culture are those familiar throughout Greece.

But for all this "Greekness", Santorini remains a special place and its inhabitants possess a special manner. Their history, for instance -- and not only its deep past but the more immediate present -- has had a special impact. And not in the usual sense of history as human-made events: the history of Santorini has been inextricably involved with nature. Thus, since the earthquake of 1956, and despite its toll, most Santorinians have stayed and rebuilt - even expanding further in developing everything from cisterns to gift shops. Such a history must produce a people with a special attitude toward the future. Perhaps some sense of the impermanence of life explains the great number of churches and chapels around the island: there are at least 250 for a population of about 7,000.

Certainly there is a special feeling generated by the environment of Santorini. It is there in the terrain, the landscape, in the very air you breathe and the light you see with -- something intense, unreal, otherworldly. Santorini is one of those places where many things you take for granted are suddenly forced into your consciousness: the basic means of transportation, for instance, or even the water you drink. It is one of those environments, too, that inspire ruminations on such matters as why human beings choose to continue to live literally atop volcanoes. What this all adds up to is the creation of a certain subdued quality to Santorini and its inhabitants. Perhaps this restraint is to compensate for the fact that underneath them is one of the more dynamic terrains on which human beings live. In any case, the isolated Santorinians are a peculiar mixture of independence and interdependence, a delicate balance that has survived thanks to the quiet respect traditionally exchanged between the islanders and visitors.

Today that balance seems threatened by the sheer volume of foreigners and touristic enterprises: each has as much right as another to be there, but they add up to a distracting presence, especially when a cruise ship deposits hundreds of tourists on the little town of Fira or when hundreds of young backpackers descend on the same few buses and beaches. Yet Santorini still manages to retain something that defies modern tourism. It is not another Mykonos, for instance, or a Hydra: those who like to feell they're part of some Chic Set should probably not go all the way to Santorini. It's an understated, low-keyed, slightly un-stylish island, where the pace is set by donkeys, a "night out" means dawdling over a meal, a resort is a beach of volcanic sand, and the "in" sound is the wind. In short, Santorini is a place where everything and everyone are finally secondary to nature. It would be nice to keep a few such places in this world.

A view of Fira.

The many names of Santorini

It is fitting that there should be some confusion over the various names associated with Santorini: there have been so many changes in the physical features of the island, so many different historical phases, that there are reflected in the many names. It seems worthwhile to take a moment to get these names spelled out here.

The many names associated with the volcanoes and the geological history of the island and its islets are described elsewhere (pp. 40-48). As to what it was actually called by early Aegeans and its first settlers (p. 49), of course, we cannot know for sure; we are dependent on the later, Classic world of literacy. By that time, tradition claimed the island's first name was *Stronghili* - "round island": this would seem to refer to the island before the great explosion of about 1500 B.C., but not necessarily, because even today there remains the impression of a curved island. Another tradition says that early settlers called it *Kalliste* - "most beautiful island" - but this sounds vaguely like chauvinism.

With the coming of the Dorians by at least 900 B.C. (see pp. 55-58), the island assumed the name of Thera in honor of the leader of the Dorian colony, Theras. Certainly this is the name by which the island passed into history, first among the ancient Greeks and then among the Romans and Byzantine Greeks. Yet even then, especially during the post-classic age, the island was known by various other names according to various sources: *Kalauria, Philiteri, Rheneia, Teusia, Theramene.* (It was also known as "Devil's Island" because of its volcanic associations).

In the twelfth century of the Christian Era, a new name for the island surfaces: Ayia Ireni. This is how it was referred to by the famous Arab geographer, Edrisi, for instance, in 1154. This name was derived from a church on the island named after Saint Irene from Thessaloniki, in northern Greece; she was said to have died in exile on the island in A.D. 304. It has never been entirely settled, however, where this church was located; some say at Perissa (p. 153), other say near Cape Riva, on Thirasia (p. 183). In any case, the name was corrupted by the Venetians and other

A detail of a typical house of Santorini.

foreigners who passed through, and it was the Italian corruption - Santorini - "Saint Irene" - that became affixed to maps.

The came the Turks, who took over the island in the sixteenth century (p. 64). Among themselves they called it *Deimerjdik* - "little mill" - evidently in reference to the many windmills around the island, but the name Santorini remained current among Europeans. In the twentieth century the Greeks officially renamed it Thera, but the name Santorini had become so generally known that it tends to survive - even in many official Greek publications.

Now, to further complicate matters, there is more than one island involved. Santorini, as Thera before it, is used to refer to largest island as well as to the group as a whole; the second largest is known as Thirasia. Meanwhile, the largest and best known town of the main island is now known as Fira (Phira), but it too has been called Thera or Tyra. In any case, Fira is simply a corruption of Thera. (In a similar case, "Candia" under the Venetians was applied both to the island of Crete as a whole and to its major city - present-day Iraklion). And finally, there is the archaeological site known as Ancient Thera: the Dorian Greeks evidently knew this major settlement as well as the island by the name of Thera.

When we consider these possible confusions over "Thera", it seems all the more sensible to refer to both the main island and the group as a whole as "Santorini". Except at those points where another precise name is called for historically, or where a specific small island is intended, this will be the practice in this book.

The church of Episkopi.

23

Santorini and Lost Atlantis

Sooner or later, all who profess to know something about Santorini must confront the question: Isn't this the island that inspired the story of lost Atlantis?'' This is a question that has been asked with increasing frequency and urgency since the discovery of the remains at Akrotiri in 1967; indeed, each year since has seen many people who come to Santorini precisely because they feel they are visiting the site of Atlantis.

Now, how to answer the sincere questioners and earnest searchers? It is all to easy - especially in a book like this, one that does not lay claim to "hard-core" scholarship - just to say, "Yes, yes - Santorini is Atlantis found!" This keeps the pro-Atlantists happy, while the anti–Atlantists could probably not care less. But this would be condescending. And moreover, quite aside from the disputes over Santorini's qualifications as Atlantis, simply agreeing avoids all the truly interesting ins-and-outs of the age-old complex question: this has already filled many hundreds of volumes. But let us at least pay the question the respect of a brief examination of the evidence as it relates to Santorini.

About the only evidence that all disputants agree on is that the first account of Atlantis is in two of Plato's dialogues, the *Timaeus* and the *Critias*, composed sometime about 360 B.C. In these works, the speaker describes a once-great center of civilization, Atlantis, that was overwhelmed by a cataclysmic disaster and sank beneath the waves. Plato's narrator provided many details of this civilization, but the most relevant for us - and the ones that vex all searchers for Atlantis - are these:

1) This took place nine thousand years earlier.

2) Atlantis was a vast island-continent.

3) It was located outside the Pillars of Hercules, which in Plato's day was understood to refer to the Strait of Gibralter.

Except for a few mystics and extremists, almost everyone who is serious about searching for Atlantis is willing to concede that the civilization Plato attributes to Atlantis could not possibly have existed nine thousand years before he was writing - approximately 9500 B.C. Nothing that is known or

Little Kaimeni.

surmised about the state of culture in that era can accept the metals, the ships, buildings, the domesticated horses, let alone the general level of society and commerce in Plato's Atlantis. So it seems easier and necessary to concede that somehow an error crept into the date; there are many complicated explanations for how this came about, but we need only accept that it is far more reasonable to believe that nine *hundred* was intended: this would place the end of Atlantis close to 1500 B.C. (Even then, many problems remain: for example, if we are to take all of Plato's details literally, no people at that time possessed the triremes - the triple-ranked oared ships - attributed to Atlantis).

As for the size of Atlantis, it is also generally conceded that the vast dimensions were an error in transmitting figures. Otherwise we are faced with accepting that a land mass about the size of Greenland sank beneath the waves and left no traces, a claim that runs absolutely against all geological knowledge. It seems better to accept that Atlantis was a largish island or group of islands and not to become too committed to its precise dimensions.

As for its location "outside the Pillars of Hercules", if we are to take Plato literally, Atlantis would have had to be somewhere off in the Atlantic Ocean; if we take him figuratively, however, he was simply saying it was located "way off there, where we don't know too much about the territory." Those who want to site Atlantis in or around the Mediterranean, of course, face a special problem, since this *was* the one region that was well known to the ancients. But the general way around this is to claim that since Plato's version is said to be based on an Egyptian account and the Egyptians were not especially a sea-faring people, the expression "beyond the Pillars of Hercules" may be interpreted as meaning simply someplace beyond the immediate coastal region of the Egyptian Delta and outside the area normally frequented by Egyptian mariners.

So, in order to keep Santorini's candidacy alive, let us accept these three "cases": Atlantis was probably an island or group of islands; possibly it was located in the Mediterranean Sea; and it may have vanished as a center of culture about 1500 B.C. If these are accepted as working hypotheses, then Santorini does seem to be a legitimate candidate. But it must also be said that once you start adjusting the "facts" of Plato's account of Atlantis to accommodate one place, you have to allow others to stretch the facts for their favorite candidates. Indeed, that is exactly what has been happening over the centuries since Plato set down the story of Atlantis: there is hardly a point on the face of the earth that someone or other has not claimed as the location of Atlantis. To discuss this would be a book in itself: the fascinating story of how people have sought Atlantis for the last 2,300 years. All we can say here is that those who insist on claiming that Santorini is, once and for all, "Atlantis found", must recognize that their greatest arguments will be not with the non-believers, the anti-Atlantists, but with other true-believers. Just to cite one instance, in 1973 a fair amount of publicity was generated by a group of people who claimed to have located Atlantis just off the southwestern coast of Spain. Presumably they were as sincere and knowledgeable as those who believe that Santorini is *the* authentic site of Atlantis.

This said, it does seem that Santorini has come into focus in recent years as an extremely strong candidate for the chief inspirer, if not the literal site, of lost Atlantis. The suggestion that Santorini was the site of Atlantis seems to have first been made in 1872 by a Frenchman, Louis Figuier, writing in his book, *La terre et les mers;* he was influenced by the finds on Santorini made by some fellow Frenchmen only a few years earlier (p. 139), but he had very little else to go on except an inspired hunch. The claim that Atlantis had been located in the eastern Mediterranean was repeated by various people, but they had little or no evidence to advance their assertions. But in 1909, another candidate was put forward by a young British scholar, K.T. Frost: influenced by the recent spectacular finds on Crete, he suggested that Minoan Crete had been the site and source of the Atlantis civilization. Frost, moreover, was able to point out several striking parallels between Plato's Atlantis, and Minoan Crete, such as:

1) The advanced engineering and architectural achievements.
2) The extent of the "empire" over several other islands.
3) The (relatively) sudden end due (apparently) to some catastrophe.

From that point on, Minoan Crete remained one of the strongest candidates, and even highly respectable archaeologists and scholars were willing to speculate that possibly elements of Minoan culture and history had passed - by word of mouth in Greece, possibly by writing in Egypt - into Plato's age to shape his version. Then, with the discovery of the site at Akrotiri in 1967, and each successive year's finds, a new possibility suggested itself (and the world's popular media picked it up almost immediately as though it were a certainty): Santorini's volcanic explosion had wiped out both the island's own settlements and the major Minoan centers on Crete, making Santorini if not the actual center of the Atlantis civilization, at least the source of its reputation as a sunken island.

And taking a reasonably flexible view of Plato's account, Santorini does seem to fulfill several conditions. True, it was never a vast continent, but the thirty-three square miles of land that sank beneath the sea was probably the largest mass that anyone then - or since - has known to sink. And the great cataclysm that occurred at Santorini about 1500 B.C. would certainly have impressed the inhabitants of the eastern Mediterranean - Greek-speaking, Egyptian, and many others. Furthermore, it was just far enough back in time to become legendary yet close enough in history to be transmitted, one way or another, by one people or another.

As for the level of culture, although there is no indication that Santorini possessed most of the things that Plato attributes to Atlantis - the great harbor installations, for instance, let alone the horse race course! - the site at Akrotiri is now revealing that Santorini did share in some of the elements of the Minoan civilization. Then, if we take the geological aspects of Santorini and the cultural elements of Minoan Crete and assume that these became joined and confused in the stories and lore that got passed down over the centuries, Santorini - Crete meets some of the general requirements. There are even a number of specific details in Plato's account that coincide suprisingly with known elements of the Santorini-Crete world:

1) The advanced hydraulic and plumbing system of Atlantis - with hot and cold "running water" - can be paralleled in the Minoan Palaces (and possibly reflects volcanic vents on Santorini).

2) White, black, and red stonework characterized the structures of Atlantis - and these three colors are prominent in the cliffs of Santorini.

3) The significance of bulls in the ritual life and the method of capturing them (with staves and nooses) are similar for Atlantis and Minoan Crete.

Well, some people are content to stop their search for Atlantis at this point and shout "Eureka!". But if you really want to make a serious investigation, you must realize that for every such detail that seems to be literally parallel, there is at least another detail of Plato's account that, if taken literally, would rule out Santorini and Crete. Aside from the major objections dealt with earlier - the date, size, and location - these include such points as:

1) There were said to be many elephants on Atlantis.

2) Thousands of horse-drawn war chariots were employed in warfare.

3) And when Atlantis sank, it left nothing but a shoal of mud.

To conclude - for a book of this sort has space for only the most cursory essay on the Atlantis question - we have tried to focus on this matter of Santorini's relation to Atlantis. Pages can be filled discussing various ancient myths, legends, poems, traditions, and historical and geographical allusions that seem to place Atlantis in the Aegean world. But in the end, what it all comes around to is not so much a problem of geologial,

Approaching Santorini.

geographical, historical or other forms of evidence as one of considering how a great mind like Plato's worked. If you feel he was being literal - reporting the actual words of one of his colleagues (Critias), who was in turn reporting the actual words of an ancestor (Solon), who was in turn reporting the words he heard from some Egyptian priests, who in turn were reporting a story that had been passed down by their ancestors of many centuries earlier - then you will believer that Atlantis is to be found in some geographical site. And Santorini (with or without Crete) provides as likely a homeland as any.

But if you feel that Plato was drawing upon deep sources of the imagination - sources that, to be sure, drew upon an understanding of how the physical world functions and how history has often transpired and how human beings behave - then you will believe that, although Atlantis may never be geographically located, Santorini conforms with the ideal of a lost world as well as any place. In either case, then, you can relax and let Santorini become your "Atlantis Found!"

Burnt Isle Foreground, Fira in background.

The Environment
The Cycladic World

Along with possessing many names, Santorini can also be thought of as belonging to several "families". It is, of course, an Aegean island, one of the many that stud the great sea of that name, bounded on the west and north by Greece, on the east by Turkey, and on the south by Crete. This area has also been known through history - and still is in several European languages - as the Archipelago, a name that means "chief sea" but which came to be applied to the islands thereon.

Today, politically speaking, Santorini belongs to a Greek Nome (something like a French prefecture) called the Cyclades, which includes some thirty islands and islets, about twenty of which are inhabited. The capital of this Nome is at Ermoupolis on Syros, and along with that island and Santorini, the Cyclades include: Amorgos, Anafi, Andros, Delos, Folegandros, Ios, Kea, Kimolos, Kithnos, Milos, Mykonos, Naxos, Paros, Serifos, Sifnos, Sikinos, Tinos, and others. But the Cyclades (from a Greek word meaning "circle": everyone should recognize our "cycle") in ancient times were only some twelve to fifteen islands viewed as encircling the tiny island of Delos, birthplace of Apollo and Artemis and one of the most sacred territories of the ancient Greek world. By a strictly traditional interpretation, then, Santorini is not a Cycladic island but belongs to the Southern Sporades ("scattered"), one of three island-groups (the other being the Northern and Eastern Sporades) that were seen as scattered around the Cyclades.

Aside from these historical and political aspects, Santorini has come to be seen as a Cycladic island, a species, or at least subspecies, of the Mediterranean island world. The ancients had several tales to explain how the Cyclades came to be there. Callimachos, the Alexandrian Greek poet of the third century B.C., said that Poseidon, in a rage, "planted these islands firmly in the abyss of the deep so that they would forget the land". Of course Callimachos was one who called all Cretans liars, but still his harsh judgement probably reflects the harshness of life on these islands, then if not now.

There is another, more dramatic story to account for Santorini in the tale of the voyage of the Argonauts. While in North Africa, a local deity, Triton, gave them a clod of earth before they set forth on their homeward journey. Sailing through the sea north of Crete, one Luphemus threw the clod of earth overboard, and the island of Kalliste, or Santorini, rose up on that spot.

However, Santorini and the other Cyclades islands got where they are (p. 40), their inhabitants to this day retain some sense of difference from their fellow Greeks; sometimes, in fact, the islanders claim to be of "purer" Greek strain, although it is hard to imagine that among the many transients in this island world that there was not some "leakage". Such considerations aside, the Cycladic world does seem to be characterized by certain elements: an intense light, limpid air, and dry atmosphere; white houses and chapels against blue skies and rocky slopes; small harbors ringed with fishing boats and cafés; fine beaches and rough trails; old windmills and abandoned forts; golden vineyards and silvery olive groves; bracing legends and chilling myths; archaeological remains that seem to be part of the natural world; historical memories that seem to be part of modern life. It is this Cycladic Santorini that people travel to experience.

Fira as seen from the sea.

The Geographic Setting

Santorini lies in the Aegean Sea about 130 miles from Piraeus (and 115 miles from Cape Sounion, the outermost point of Attica), 60 miles from Mykonos, and 68 miles from Crete. The total area of the islands comprising the Santorini group is about thirty-six square miles. The largest island, Santorini (or Thera), is about twenty-nine square miles: Thirasia is about four square miles; Aspronisi ("white island") is about 50,000 square yards (or some ten acres); the remaining three square miles are formed by Palea ("old") and Nea ("new") Kaimeni, the "Burnt Isles". Santorini, Thirasia, and Aspronisi are what remain of the great explosion of about 1500 B.C. (pp. 40-46): the Burnt Isles are what exist at present after the series of eruption since that explosion (pp. 46-48).

The great inner bay of water covers an area of about thirty-three square miles, with a circumference of about twenty miles. Its rim of land is broken by about one mile of water at the north-west corner – between Santorini and Thirasia – and by about three miles of water in the southwest, with tiny Aspronisi in the middle. This great salt-water "lake" is actually the caldera of the former volcanic island that extended over the total area. Note: this is, in the technical language of vulcanologists, a caldera (from the Spanish for "kettle"), not a crater or cone: a caldera is a steep-sided basin left after the subsidence that follows an eruption or series of eruptions (and, in this case, the subsequent engulfment with water).

The water in this caldera-bay is now from about 600 to 1,280 feet deep, with the deepest point just west of Palea Kaimeni. Directly off the port of Fira, the depth drops sharply to about 600 feet, which means that large ships that come in close must tie up to buoys permanently chained to the sea floor. Large ships can, however, anchor somewhat further off on a point (known as *Bangos*), where an underwater mountain peak forms a shallows about 100 feet deep.

The main island of Santorini is distinguished by the high cliffs that form its west side, an elliptical rim or crescent that arcs about fifteen miles from north to south. These cliffs rise from about 200 to 1,100 feet, with Fira, the main town, at a height of about 800 feet. The various types of material (slag, cinders, lava, pumice, earth) - laid down mostly by the eruption of 1500 B.C. - have formed these cliffs with their multicolored layers - red, black, white, gray, brown, and others - that serve as a cross-section of history, geology, and time itself.

Santorini's caldera has led it to be compared (in size, structure, and general geological history) to Crater Lake, in the State of Oregon, USA, but the island as a whole might better be compared to St. Vincent in the Caribbean: before the great explosion, Santorini probably looked much like St. Vincent. A volcanic cone rose at its center to a height of about 5,340 feet; that collapsed, leaving the remaining land on the main island of Santorini and on Thirasia to slope down toward the outer sea. This slope on the main island is broken by several peaks that are remnants of the original island - before the great explosion - These include: Profitis Elias, highest point on Santorini at 1,863 feet; Mesa Vouno, the site of Ancient Thera (p. 159), 1,211 feet; Megalo Vouno, in the north, 1,092 feet; and the little "lonely stone", Monolithos, which rises to about 100 feet along the east coast (p. 154).

View from Nea Kaimeni.

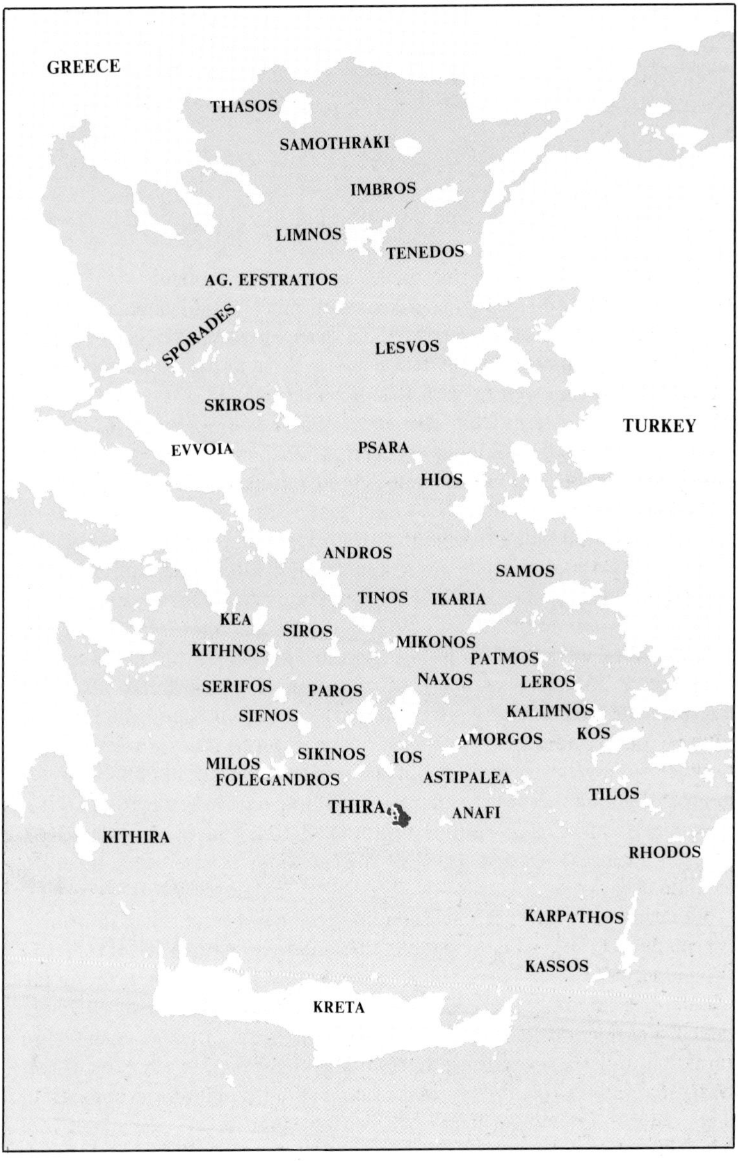
GREECE
THASOS
SAMOTHRAKI
IMBROS
LIMNOS
TENEDOS
AG. EFSTRATIOS
SPORADES
LESVOS
SKIROS
TURKEY
EVVOIA
PSARA
HIOS
ANDROS
SAMOS
TINOS
IKARIA
KEA
SIROS
KITHNOS
MIKONOS
PATMOS
SERIFOS
PAROS
NAXOS
LEROS
SIFNOS
KALIMNOS
AMORGOS
KOS
MILOS
SIKINOS
IOS
FOLEGANDROS
ASTIPALEA
TILOS
THIRA
ANAFI
KITHIRA
RHODOS
KARPATHOS
KASSOS
KRETA

The Elements

It is typical of Santorini that the traditional four elements – air, water, earth, fire – should still figure in life on this elemental island.

Air: Somehow the wind seems to be a special presence on Santorini; the straightforward physical explanation has to do with the island's location, size, and shape as well as with the prevailing winds of this part of the Mediterranean. Aside from the generally prevailing north wind (the *etesian*), there is the infamous *meltemi*, a north wind that blows rather stiffly and steadily from about mid-July to mid-September; its side-effect, though, is to make the otherwise torrid heat of those weeks bearable. But it must be admitted that although the atmosphere on Santorini is especially fresh, invigorating, brisk, it can also get damn windy and chilly.

In addition, the wind has left two special imprints on the landscape. One are the many windmills that now stand all over the island. Up until quite recently, they were used for grinding grains like barley, but now they are abandoned, like lost sentinels of the past. The wind has also had considerable effect on the construction of dwellings on Santorini. For one, houses have traditionally huddled close together for protection; for another, houses have a curved roof, a kind of barrel vault, that is said to act as a natural air conditioner – making a building cool in summer and warm in winter. This curved roof is reproduced today in modern materials (namely, cement) – as in many of the buildings erected since the 1956 earthquake.

Water: Water has become something of a problem on Santorini – especially as more and more people, foreigners and natives, want to live in the modern manner. There are no lakes, ponds, rivers, or streams on the island; there are only a few springs – the chief fresh-water one being over near Kamari - and well water is usually brackish. As there is virtually no rainfall during the several months from May to September, every bit of rain water that falls during the rest of the year is saved; communities collect it in large cisterns, individuals in barrels. This valuable water is needed not only for drinking and domestic used but also for irrigation of crops (although

View from Fira looking to southern end of island.

Coastline of Santorini's caldera.

remember that vegetation gets much of its moisture from the condensation of the humid atmosphere).

In the earthquake of 1956, so many cisterns were damaged that the government had to help build large, solid cisterns for all the island's communities. This still leaves a growing demand for water, especially in Fira; this has been met in recent years by the constant trucking of water from one or another of the island's springs; although it should be conserved, you will always have potable fresh water; if there is ever any doubt, you can always order bottled water.

Earth: What is surprising about a volcanic island like Santorini is not how little is grown there but that anything can be grown. In fact, volcanic ash makes quite a good soil for growing certain crops, particularly some varieties of grapes and tomatoes. The grapes are used in making the island's two well-known wines, the *visanto* and *nichteri* (p. 92); the tomatoes are used in making tomatoe paste. There are, however, relatively few trees on the island.

What agriculture there is is conducted principally on the sweeping slopes and plains along the eastern and southern sides of the main island. It also involves terracing with dry-stone walls. The main crops are barley (and if you happen to be there at the harvest season, you'll see them threshing by age-old methods); the fava, a kind of broad bean (used to make a delicious soup); and pistachio nuts (recently introduced as a cash crop).

Fire: There is a poetic justice that this island which has suffered so much from its fiery bowels should turn around and extract some economic benefits from the volcano's activity. In fact, what the Santorinians exploit is the ejected material from the great eruption of about 1500 B.C. (p. 42-46), for the main industry of Santorini is the mining of pumice and volcanic ash. (Practically the only other industries are some handicraft trades – leather-working, rug-making. Beyond that, the people of Santorini - especially in Fira – have long cut their homes, sheds, roads, and other structures right out of the volcanic "bedrock", as well as using it for terraces and cultivating its ash. And to round out this irony, it was the extraction of some of this volcanic material back in the 1860s – to help in making the Suez Canal – that led to the chance discovery of the first Minoan-era remains that, by a number of steps, have led to the discovery of the great Akrotiri site (pp. 138-141).

As described elsewhere (p. 42), there were two major types of material thrown up by the great Bronze Age eruptions and explosion. First came the pumice, a variety of volcanic glass full of tiny cavities; this blanketed much of the island in a layer thirteen to seventeen feet thick. Then, with the explosion of the great central core of the island, masses of ash known as tephra (p. 42) were ejected; this fell over the island during the period that must have lasted many months, accumulating to a thickness of 70 to 200 feet – and in one area, 217 feet.

The pressure of the huge layer of tephra over the centuries somewhat solidified the lower level of pumice. The pumice is thus harder as well as coarser than the tephra, and slightly more difficult to mine; it is also a more expensive material, but it is wanted for bricks, insulation, cleaning and polishing, and other industrial uses. Pumice is recognizable as a porous, whitish stone that floats for some time on the surface of water; occasionally large masses are seen adrift in the sea around Santorini. Sometimes the locals will call it "porcelain" in a desire to "translate" it into English, but this is a case of mistaken identity: this is a confusion with the Italian *pozzuolana*, the name for a type of volcanic ash mined near Naples and used in making cement.

And it is the second layer at Santorini, the tephra, that is the relative of this *pozzuolana*. The Santorini tephra is used with lime to make a cement that – because of its imperviousness to water, and resistance to sea water – is especially valued for harbor installations. The Santorini tephra is a quite white, powdery material, soft enough so that it can be extracted by hand. It also happens to be rather elastic and does not break suddenly; this property allows for it to be removed in an unusual way.

Workmen dig horizontal tunnels into the lower layers of the tephra; once within, they dig a series of cross-connecting tunnels, forming a vast subterranean grid. This weakens the overhead layer, and after some weeks, experienced workmen can sense when the roof is about to collapse. All the workmen leave the tunnels at this point and wait for the collapse of the cliff of ash; it is then removed in its powdery form and dropped down large chutes to fill the holds of ships waiting alongside. (The main quarry is just south of Fira, but there are other operations around Santorini, including one on the northwest tip, just behind Oia.)

Incidentally, it was tephra's elastic property that first led Professor Marinatos to consider that he would excavate at Akrotiri with tunnels and then leave the site as a kind of "underground Pompeii" (p. 131). Another characteristic – that is hardens so upon contact with water – has allowed the people of Santorini to dig a room into it and then go over the walls with a wet brush or cloth, forming a surface impermeable to air or moisture and one that keeps dust from falling.

The Geological History of Santorini

There are times when we envy the ancients their ability to explain things with myths and gods: it is so simple and straightforward. Certainly one such time is when we come to explain the geological history of Santorini. We cannot take this approach, but we can at least try to make the geological history clear by breaking it down into a series of phases. (Even then we must keep in mind that it has actually been a more dynamic process, and that not all the authorities agree on every detail.)

(1) Many hundreds of thousands of years ago, the area of Santorini and the other Aegean islands, including Crete, was not a sea but a continuous land mass – broken by some lake basins – that joined the continents of Europe and Asia. This land mass has been called Aegeis. Gradually most of this land area subsided – say, by about 1,000,000 years ago (quite recently, geologically speaking, but certainly not in the same time-frame as Plato's Atlantis: p. 24). Sea water moved in to cover the great plateau, and all that was left above the surface were the higher peaks – which we know today as the Aegean islands. The highest point (excluding Crete) is on Naxos (3,286 feet), while the submerged plateau is about 300 to 650 feet below the surface.

(2) Santorini at this time was nothing but a few small rocky peaks, perhaps forming a total of only some five square miles, formed mainly of metaphoric schist, marble, and andesite. The peaks included those we know today as Profitis Elias, Mesa Vouno, Monolithos, Athinios, and Platinamos, as well as a few other small projections. But this was an unstable, geologically active area, and there occurred a series of eruptions and lava flows from submarine volcanoes. The ejected matter filled in the area around the peaks and built up a quite large island with a conical mountain more or less at its center. All this, of course, took many thousands of years.

(3) Then, about 25,000 B.C. there occurred a so-called paroxysmal (or violent) eruption of the volcano underneath the island. This ejected masses of ashes all over the eastern Mediterranean, from Sicily to Asia Minor (as

Volcanic ash removed to make cement.

indicated by deep-sea cores). (The technical name for such volcanic ash, by the way, is tephra, the Greek word for "ashes"); it denotes all the light materials ejected in a volcanic eruption – cinders, dust, pumice, as well as what we would recognize as ashes.) At the same time, the central cone of the island collapsed, leaving a greatly fragmented island; exactly what its shape was, though, is not known.

(4) There then began a repetition of a process similar to that which had built up the previous island: a series of eruptions from various active cones, throwing up lava, stones, tephra, etc. that filled in the area once again. The result eventually was a relatively round island of about 70 square miles in area; more or less in the center was a conical peak about 3,500 feet high, while elsewhere were other lesser peaks (including the original ones such as Profitis Elias, etc.).

(5) This island then became quiescent, so that the inhabitants of this part of the world – once they happened to venture this far into the Aegean - would probably have had no idea that it was a dormant volcano. The volcanic ash itself, what with the humus that had gradually settled over the island, was fertile enough to allow trees and other vegetation to take hold. (Volcanic ash from this period preserves fossilized leaves from palm and olive trees). Whatever its reputation or appeal, the island seems to have attracted its first human settlers about 3000 B.C. (p. 49). Traditionally these were the Carians (from southwest Turkey); traditionally, too, they were succeeded by Minoans (p. 50). But whatever the origins and relations of the island's inhabitants, they built up a quite prosperous and advanced culture, if Akrotiri is a fair witness (p. 150).

(6) Because of the unstable conditions that still prevailed, by about 1500 B.C. there began a series of subterranean explosions, earthquakes, and eruptions that climaxed in a convulsive, or paroxysmal, eruption: the magma chambers (magma being the molten rock) below the central cone of the island collapsed, the whole central crust of the island suddenly subsided, and the sea rushed in. This is the catastrophe responsible for the destruction of the Akrotiri and other contemporary settlements on Santorini (and possibly some on Crete: p. 150). Exactly when this occurred is still in some question, but it seems to have been about 1475 B.C. (based on radioactive carbon dating of objects from the remains). Also in question is how much time elapsed between the first warning earthquakes (and minor eruptions) and the final catastrophe; the thinking now is that a very brief time elapsed – perhaps only a few months, possibly a year or so, but certainly not many years.

(7) What is known is that some thirty-three square miles – almost half the island – collapsed, leaving the great cavity, or caldera, that filled with sea water. The remaining land masses were the outer edges of the former island: Santorini around the east, and at this time still joined to Thirasia on the northwest; and the tiny islet of Aspronisi in the southwest. Before the final collapse, but after a major earthquake, eruptions threw up first a mass of relatively coarse pumice, which laid down a layer some 13 to 17 feet thick. A series of tremors, earthquakes, and minor eruptions followed, laying down another layer of ash and pumice: an eruption then began to hurl forth great boulders and a mass of dusty volcanic tephra that covered the whole island; before it stopped, this "rain" had deposited a layer some 66 to 220 feet over Santorini. And the tephra was ejected so high into the atmosphere that it was carried by the winds and deposited in detectable amounts (as measured by deep-sea cores) over an area some 120,000 square miles – mainly to the southeast of Santorini because of the prevailing winds. Some of this tephra has been found as far as 440 miles from Santorini; one core reveals a layer of some 83 inches (this was found near the island of Karpathos, 90 miles from Santorini); a core off northeast Crete was 30 inches thick.

(8) These massive deposits of tephra mainly resulted from the final stage of the eruption, when the magma chambers were exhausted by violent explosions and the great central core of the island subsided. But such a collapse was also accompanied by other phenomena – particularly by seismic waves (also known as tsunamis) or tremendous size and force that moved across the Mediterranean Sea. Leaving Santorini at a height estimated at about 670 feet, one wave is thought to have struck Anafi, the small island just 19 miles east of Santorini, with a height of about 830 feet. Even by the time it hit Jaffa (on Israel's coast, near Tel Aviv), some 560 miles away, one wave is estimated to have been at least 25 feet high. The energy involved in this great explosion has been estimated and expressed in various ways: 100 times higher than the annual average of the earth's volcanic energy; equal to 1,000 atomic bombs (of the 1954 Bikini variety); as 600,000,000,000 kilowatt hours of energy. It dwarfs such other well-known volcanic eruptions as that of Vesuvius in A.D. 79, when Pompei was covered, or that of Mt. Pelée on Martinique in 1902. Indeed, the Santorini explosion can hardly be compared to any phenomenon known to have occurred during the span of recorded human life.

(9) Yet there is one other volcanic eruption that is similar enough to be instructive in understanding Santorini; that is the late-nineteenth century eruption of Krakatoa. Krakatoa is a small islet in the Strait of Sunda

between Java and Sumatra. After some 203 years of inactivity, it began to experience earthquakes in May, 1883. Then, on 26-27 August, a series of violent explosions resulted in some 9 square miles of Krakatoa's land mass disappearing into the air and sea. This left a great cavity some 670 to 1.000 feet into which rushed the Indian Ocean. (Because the Krakatoa explosion was of the same type as the Santorini one, this cavity is also technically a caldera: p. 33). The resultant seismic waves – some up to 100 feet high – swept across that area: a wave 55 feet high was reported at a lighthouse some 55 miles away; good-sized ships were carried miles inland. Worst of all, the waves destroyed nearly 300 towns and villages on the surrounding coasts of Java and Sumatra, killing about 36,000 people. The explosions were heard from Ceylon to Australia – over 2,000 miles away; atmospheric shock waves travelled $3^1/_2$ times around the globe – breaking windows up to 100 miles away. Masses of floating pumice – some up to 13 feet in diameter – blocked harbors and filled the sea in Sunda Strait for months afterwards; ships over a wide area of the Indian Ocean reported pumice in large quantities. Meanwhile, a pall of darkness spread east and west up to 150 miles in each direction – the ejected volcanic material. Fine dust particles blew off as far as 1,000 miles; some got into the stratosphere and were carried around the world for months; since volcanic ash consists of minute crystals of pure glass that reflect the sun's rays, this created superb sunsets throughtout the world (so blazingly spectacular that fire engines were called out in Poughkeepsie, New York, and New Haven, Connecticut).

(10) Now, consider that all this is known to have resulted from a volcanic explosion involving the subsidence of a mass of land only about one-fourth the size of Santorini's subsidence, and that Krakatoa's eruption deposited only a few inches of an ash blanket (as oppossed to up to 220 feet in places on Santorini). Then imagine what an impact the Santorini explosion might have had not only on Santorini but on other Aegean islands. And indeed, there is some confirmation on places such as Anafi and Keos – and, most suggestive of all, on Crete. There is strong reason to believe that the cataclysm that overwhelmed so many of the Minoan sites on Crete about this same time – Amnissos (pp. 141), Knossos, Nirou, Malia, Mokhlos and Psira, Gournia, Vathypetro, Arkhanes, and even Kato Zakros (p. 46) – was at least related to the earthquake(s) associated with the Santorini explosion, and possibly due to the fall-out and seismic waves. The evidence of the seismic waves is circumstantial, but the evidence of an earthquake at Minoan sites on Crete is clear; while as we have seen, (p. 28), deep-sea cores establish that large quantities of volcanic ash fell on places far more distant

Santorini coast reveals layers of volcanic ash.

Volcanic rocks Nea Kaimeni.

45

Removing volcanic ash (tephra) to make cement.

from Santorini than even the farthest site on Crete, Kato Zakros. The rain of ashes over the fields of Crete would have had a drastic impact on the agriculture of the Minoans – indeed, on their survival, what with eye, skin, lung, and other disorders. Presumably many Minoans would have left at least the central and eastern settlements most affected – some heading for inland sites, some for the west of the island, and some to the Greek mainland, especially to the Peloponnesos, where they would have joined the Mycenaean world. And in fact there was, about this time, a decline of Minoan culture and a rise of the Mycenaeans; although Knossos revived, it seems to have been under the control of Mycenaeans. (As for whether any of this has a bearing, direct or otherwise on the tale of "lost Atlantis", this is discussed on pp. 24-30).

(11) Following this great paroxysmal eruption, what remained of the island gradually became quiescent; humus settled over the ash, and once again it became populated with vegetation, animal life – and eventually by humans (pp. 52). After some centuries, there began another series of explosions, eruptions, earthquakes, and related phenomena that have somewhat changed the appearance of Santorini; not all of the early catastrophes can be definitely dated or accepted by all authorities, but we list them as they are generally agreed to have occurred.

(12) 236 B.C.: There is said to have been volcanic activity that finally separated Thirasia from northwest Santorini.

(13) 197 B.C.: An eruption that went on some four days in the sea between Santorini (main island) and Thirasia produced a small islet; the Rhodians who investigated it called it Iera ("holy") and even dedicated an altar to Poseideon there. But it is now known as Palea Kaimeni ("old burnt isle") to distinguish it from the later, the larger, Nea Kaimeni. Over the centuries, too, other eruptions added to this islet, so that it now ries to some 300 feet.

(14) A.D. 19 (or 46): A tiny islet, known as Thira, appeared in the caldera as a result of an eruption, but this eventually vanished.

(15) A.D. 726: A major eruption produced pumice that reached as far as Asia Minor and Macedonia.

(16) 1570: The south coast of Santorini collapsed, and the ancient port of Eleusis sumberged (p. 152).

(17) 1573: East of Palea Kaimeni an eruption produced a small oval-shaped islet, about 220 feet high; this became known as Mikra ("small") Kaimeni.

(18) 1650: A series of earthquakes preceded a major sumbarine explosion off the northeast coast of Santorini; lava formed a small island, but the sea eventually washed most of it away, and all that is now left is a submerged reef known as Kouloumbos. But this was a major disaster in its day; seismic waves resulted in damage throughout the Aegean, and poisonous gases killed and blinded many people and animals on Santorini.

(19) 1707-11: An explosion produced an eruption of lava between Palea Kaimeni and Mikra Kaimeni that continued for some years; the resultant islet was named Nea ("new") Kaimeni.

(20) 1866-70: A series of volcanic eruptions adjecent to Nea Kaimeni produced several small islets; two vanished, leaving nothing but small reefs. But two eventually were joined by lava flows to Nea Kaimeni, leaving that islet three times larger than before. One of these was called Afroessa; the other was named George I (in honor of the King of Greece); this King George crater now forms the highest peak on Nea Kaimeni, at some 430 feet. This eruption was enough to produce pumice that was carried as far away as Crete. But it was important for another reason: it attracted Greek, French and other geologists and archaeologists who found the first traces of what would later be identified as Minoan-era Santorini: p. 183.

(21) 1925-26: A quite large explosion occurred in August 1925, and the subsequent eruption lasted till May 1926. Some 100,000,000 cubic yards of lava poured out, filling in much of the channel between Mikra Kaimeni and

Nea Kaimeni and joining them as one; this also formed the dome on Nea Kaimeni now known as "Daphne".

(22) 1928: An explosion between Mikra Kaimeni and Nea Kaimeni filled in more of the channel between Mikra and Nea Kaimeni, and formed the Nautilus and Tholos craters.

(23) 1939-41: The volcano on Nea Kaimeni was active, sending out lava during a series of eruptions and forming various domes and cavities; but aside from changing surface features, the basic isled did not alter.

(24) 1950: An explosion and eruption that lasted for about two months formed the dome known as Liatsikas on the upper slops of the King George I dome.

(25) 1956: This was a major earthquake throughout the Aegean; it registered 7.8 on the Richter scale (its center was near Amorgos) and produced destructive seismic waves. On Santorini, it killed 48 people and injured hundreds; it destroyed some 2,000 houses – essentially half the structures along the west coast of the island – and broke many of the island's cisterns.

(26) The islets of Santorini have been quiet since 1956, although there are occasional minor tremors, and hot vapors and sulfurous gases issue from the craters, fumaroles, and fissures of recent decades: for the moment, though, these receive the ultimate contempt of being treated as tourist attractions.

A History of Santorini

Santorini, we have suggested, is one of those rare places on this earth where human beings seem to play a supporting role to the natural phenomena: to this day, the geology seems to be the "star" constantly threatening to dismiss a chorus of human by-standers. As the geological drama is recounted in detail elsewhere (pp. 40-48), we shall here spotlight the human history. But one thing should be emphasized at the outset: the hard facts are few and far between and with the exception of the later periods, legend, tradition, and speculation still dominate much of the story of Santorini.

Prehistory:

The Bronze Age (c. 3000-1500 B.C.)

It is not really known for sure when the first settlers arrived on Santorini. The island had been sitting there for many thousands of years, its volcanoes dormant: humus had settled over the land and allowed a reasonable selection of flora (palm trees, for instance) and fauna to take hold Yet this fertile, round oasis did just that – sat there, while other islands on the Aegean were being settled: Crete, for instance, by about 6500 B.C.; and Milos was being exploited for its obsidian by about 7500 B.C.. Until the late 1960s, it was usually said that the first settlers on Santorini arrived about 2000 B.C., but the excavations at Akrotiri (p. 144) have changed this estimate. Although Santorini does not seem to have shared in the full Early and Middle Cycladic culture, traces at the lower levels of Akrotiri go back to the Early Cycladic Period (2600-2000 B.C.) and even into the preceeding centuries of the Chalcolithic Age (the "copper-stone" transitional culture between the Stone Age and the Bronze Age). So it now seems that the first settlers were there closer to 3000 B.C.

Who these first settlers were is still another unknown. Tradition had it that they were Carians – people from Caria, the southwestern coast of Asia Minor (now modern Turkey). It seems quite likely that these people, looking about for more territory to exploit, might have come across Santorini. And in general, it is believed that the Aegean islands were settled by peoples from Asia Minor; there is strong reason to believe that the early settlers of Crete, for instance, as well as the later waves who stimulated the Minoan culture, were from Asia Minor.

Wherever they came from, the first settlers – and any subsequent groups – must have brought some of their material culture and techniques with them to Santorini. And although during the following centuries – say, at least, 2000 to 1500 B.C. – they developed a more elaborate society and life style, their basic culture did not change that much. Most of the people were peasant-farmers who grew grains or tended olive trees; others fished, and some tended sheep and goats. Although gold and bronze were used for certain special objects, stone remained the basic material for tools. The Santorinians used the potter's wheel for making pottery, and eventually came to decorating their work with quite lovely motifs. Some of the Santorini ceramics showed up in places such as Crete, Milos, Rhodes, and Cyprus, suggesting that the Santorinians traded with these other islanders, perhaps exporting surplus grain or olive oil for needed raw materials like copper or obsidian. The Santorinians knew how to weave, and they also knew to build their houses with wooden posts inserted in the stone work – to make their walls more flexible and thus less susceptible to earthquakes.

This much of the Santorinians material culture is attested to by finds from several sites (and to be seen in such collections as those in the Thera museums or the Geological and Palaeontological Museum in Athens). But it still leaves several issues open, among them the relationship of Santorinians and their culture with other Aegeans. There is some suggestion, for instance, that the people on the island of Milos had some special relationship with Santorini – possibly sending over colonists, and certainly sending on their pottery. But one thing seems certain: the major influence on Santorinians seems to have come from the Minoan culture of Crete.

Starting at least as far back as the Early Cycladic period, Minoans were exercising some influence over their Aegean neighbors – on Cythera, for instance. Certainly by the Middle Cycladic period (2000 - 1600 B.C.), the Minoan influence was pronounced, whether through actual colonies or simple trading posts, on such islands as Keos, Miletos, or Milos: some fine frescoes at Phylakopi, the capital of Milos at that time, seem quite Minoan. Centuries later, Thucydides was to write that the Minoans displaced the Carians throughout the Cycladic world, and perhaps this is another of those instances where the tradition echoes reality. Certainly it makes sense that the Minoans would have exercised some influence over their neighbor Santorini, given the sheer size of Crete and numbers of Minoans. And although Crete could keep an eye on traffic across the southern edge of the Aegean, Santorini would be especially strategic as an outpost and jumping-off point for traffic to the north.

In any case, there is no question of Minoan relations with Santorini; what is in doubt is the exact nature of their relations. Did the Minoans at some point send up a large contingent to colonize or conquer Santorini? Or did the small island just gradually drift into orbit around its large, dynamic neighbor? The end result would probably have been about the same, as the Minoans seem to have exercised power mainly through economic rather than military means. When this was taking place is also in question. Most of the ceramics found on Santorini that show Minoan influence or are direct imports date from the period of 1600-1500 B.C., but there has been found on Santorini at least one pot with a Linear A inscription, and that would seem to push the contacts back 50 - 100 years earlier. Certainly in its final phase, the settlement at Akrotiri had strong cultural, if not political, links with Minoan Crete.

In one respect, though, the people of Akrotiri enjoyed at least equal standing with the Minoans: fresco painting. Of course nothing is really proven by the handsome frescoes at Akrotiri (pp. 118-122): they would have been painted by any number of people – local Santorinians (in turn, of any number of origins), visiting Minoans, or still third parties. All we can say is that the Akrotiri frescoes suggest a slightly independent vision – both in contents and style – from the Minoan frescoes, one that looks more toward Africa than to Crete: the antelopes, the monkeys, the exotic humans, and the whole frieze that has been interpreted as depicting an expedition in Libya (pp. 121). Whatever the Santorinians' relations with Crete, the people of Akrotiri do not seem to have been overwhelmed by the Minoans.

What did overwhelm the Santorinians, of course, was the explosion that wiped out the very core of their island home. The geological details are discussed elsewhere (pp. 40-48); also the question of this episode's relation to "lost Atlantis" is treated separately (pp. 24-30); here we shall concentrate on the impact of this phenomenon on the history of Santorini. Although there is some dispute as to exactly when it occurred – probably about 1450 B.C., or within the century before or after – there is no questions that it did occur. It is also established that the final disaster was preceded by a series of earthquakes, which knocked over most of the structure at Akrotiri – and probably all over Santorini (and possibly many on Crete). But the inhabitants returned to Akrotiri, removed the bodies of victims, cleared up some of the roads, houses, and courtyards, shored up some of the walls, set up some new workshops, and started to take up life again.

But shortly thereafter – it may have been only a few weeks, but more likely a few months – the volcano started to act up; a shower of pumice would have been enough to send everyone in flight if they had not already started to abandon their homes earlier. But since no human remains have as yet been found at Akrotiri (although some have been found elsewhere in Santorini) and since relatively few small valuables have turned up, the suggestion is that the people of Akrotiri did leave well before the great explosion. If they left the island by boats, and if they survived to land elsewhere, they must have had a good head start, because once the explosion occurred it was of such force that it was accompanied by massive seismic waves and a tremendous "rain" of tephra in that part of the eastern Mediterranean. (Although ash from Santorini had been found on Crete for many years, it was only in 1985 that scientists reported finding Santorini's volcanic ash on the northern coast of Egypt).

Transition:

Post-Explosion Santorini (c. 1400 - 900 B.C.)

Whatever the fate of the inhabitants, all human settlements on Santorini were obliterated, and given the impact of such a catastrophe on the southeastern Mediterranean world, it seems safe to assume that no one would have been tempted to try to resettle there for a long, long time. For one thing, it would take many years for the island to "cool off"; then humus, vegetation, and animal life (at least insects, birds, etc.) had to have time to get re-established. Undoubtedly sailors came close and then reported developments over the years, but Santorini certainly did not participate in the Myceneaean phase that followed the decline of the Minoans on Crete and elsewhere in the eastern Mediterranean.

The first people to settle the now halved island cannot be identified for certain. But there was a later tradition that the Phoenicians came to Santorini, and in a most particular way. Cadmus was a Phoenician prince whose sister, Europa, had been abducted by a white bull – in fact, Zeus in one of his manifestations. Cadmus set forth with a group of Phoenicians to find his sister and came to Santorini; there he left Membliaros, one of his trusty men, to lead a Phoenician colony on the island. Cadmus moved on, eventually, according to the legend, to found Thebes in Greece and to introduce the alphabet to the Greeks. Now as with such tales, there are several inconsistencies if it is to be taken at all literally. The traditional date for the founding of Thebes was 1313 B.C.; yet Europa, after being abducted by Zeus, gave birth to Minos on Crete – certainly several hundred years earlier.

But it is better not to get bogged down in such details. What seems to matter is that the Phoenicians could well have colonized Santorini. After the decline of the Mycenanaeans, the Phoenicians began to assert themselves as a trading force in the eastern Mediterranean, and if they did not get to Santorini by 1300 B.C. they may well have gotten there by about 1000 B.C. By this time, the Phoenicians were moving westward across the Mediterranean and setting up a series of trading posts along the way, the greatest of which was to become Carthage. Santorini would have appealed to the Phoenicians as a stepping-stone; since the Phoenicians did not always bother to colonized in the usual sense, they may have simply made use of the island as a port and trans-shipment station.

Dorian Santorini (c. 900-323 B.C.)

Tradition also spoke of the next colonists on Santorini, but this time archaeology confirms their presence: the Dorians, a Greek-speaking people who came from somewhere north of Greece and moved down across the Achaean - Mycenaean world from about 1200 B.C. onward. When they actually got to Santorini is not known; the date varies from 1100 to 800 B.C.; the Dorians seem to have been on Crete by at least 1000 B.C., but then they may well have by-passed Santorini; certainly tombs and pottery at Ancient Thera go back to at least 800 B.C. (The Ionians from the coasts and off-shore islands of Asia Minor were colonizing the Cyclades about this time – 1000 - 800 B.C. – but do not seem to have settled on Santorini.) But if the date of the Dorians' arrival is uncertain, there is a very specific account by Herodotus of their first settlement on Santorini.

The leader was said to have been Theras, son of Autesion, a hero of Thebes and a descedant of Cadmus, the Phoenician founder of Thebes. (In another tale, Theras is said to be a descendant of Euphemus, the Argonaut who tossed the clod of earth into the sea and that then became Santorini: p. 163). This Theras, although of Theban origins, was at Sparta where he was serving as Regent while guardian of his young nephews, the twin brothers, Procleus and Euresthenes, heirs to the Spartan throne. But when they came of age to assume the throne, Theras decided it would be too hard to subject himself to their rule, so he led a group to colonized Kalliste - as Santorini was then called. Because of his Phoenician ancestry, moreover, he is said to have maintaned good relations with the Phoenicians already on the island. In any case, the island under the Dorian Greeks assumed its new name in his honor – Thera.

As usual, there is probably a mixture of truth and fancy in this tale, but one thing is sure: by about 850 - 800 B.C., the Dorians were settled on Santorini. They came there, too, with a more or less fully realized Geometric culture – as exemplified by the oldest vases found at Ancient Thera - but once on this small, remote island they tended to become isolated and "frozen" in space and time. The Dorians did possess a strongly disciplined society, and were capable of certain superb cultural achievements such as their Doric style in architecture. But whereas the Dorians on the mainland combined with a mixture of Greek peoples and cultural influences to help create the great classical civilization, the Dorians of Santorini could never get beyond the Archaic mode.

Herodotus said that the Dorians established seven towns on Santorini, but the only one that has produced any significant remains is Ancient Thera (pp. 159). A truly ambitious community grew up there, certainly in the decades following 700 B.C., and we are fortunate to have a variety of witnesses to its activities. Many coins, for instance, have been found at Ancient Thera, dating from about 700 to 500 B.C., and some 70% of these were minted on the island of Aegina, in the Saronic Gulf, off Attica - indicative of trade links between Santorini and the mainland. In the years after 700 B.C. Ancient Thera supported a society that produced its unusual erotic and bedicatory inscriptions (p. 166). It also honored its eponymous founder with the Heroon of Theras (p. 172), and among other buildings erected a Temple of Apollo Karneios (p. 172).

Not much is actually known about the early history of Dorian Santorin, but it surfaces during the classical age in a secondary role. When Athens found itself in 480 B.C. threatened by the Persians under Xerxes, Santorini refused to join in defending the Greek mainland – and indeed even seems to have aided Xerxes. But this is understandable in that age when Santorini's distance from Greece and closeness to Asia seemed so much more significant. In the end, of course, the Greeks repulsed the Persians without the Santorinians, Then, when the Athenians formed the Delian Confederacy in 478 B.C., a league intended to include the Aegean islands, both Santorini and Milos declined to join; again, this is understable in that both these islands had been colonized by Dorians from Sparta – and the enmity between the pro-Athenian and pro-Spartan factions in Greece hardly needs explaining. (In 416 B.C., Milos became the victim of Athens' infamous punitive raid, when the island's population was slaughtered or enslaved; presumably Santorini was considered too insignificant for such treatment). By about 430 B.C., Santorini was effectively subservient to Athens; and when in 378 B.C. Athens formed its Second Maritime League, Santorini was among those who joined.

Hellenistic Santorini (323 - 146 B.C.)

By that time, Athens was no longer the power it had been, and by 338 B.C. it had succumbed to the Macedonian Greeks, led by Philip II. Then came Philip's son, Alexander the Great, who for a brief moment flashed across the stage of history, conquering an empire for the new Greece. When he died in 323 B.C., this vast empire was divided up among his generals; the most able of these was considered to be Ptolemy, and he took Egypt as the center of his mini-empire, making his capital at Alexandria, the city founded by his former leader. Under Ptolemy I Soter (who ruled from 323-285 B.C.) and his two successors, Ptolemy II Philadelphus (from 285 - 246 B.C.) and Ptolemy III Euergetes ("The Benefactor") (from 246 - 221 B.C.), Alexandria became the intellectual capital of the new Hellenistic world. Its culture represented a more cosmopolitan and sophisticated (some would say decadent) development of the old Greek civilization.

These Ptolemies - who were, remember, of Greek descent – were based in Egypt but their influence, cultural and economic if not always political and military, spread throughout the Aegean world. They erected a great sanctuary on Samothrace, finished the famous lighthouse at Rhodes, built on Delos and elsewhere; inevitably, too, they absorbed the little island of Santorini. Ptolemy I recognized its strategic value at the edge of the Aegean and when the island was treated as a naval base Ancient Thera experienced something of a revival. For a century or so it enjoyed the attentions of the Ptolemies, who erected several buildings there (pp. 161). But in 228 B.C., the Ptolemies were defeated at Andros by the Macedonians under Antigonous Doson; the Antigonids and Macedonians replaced the Ptolemies as the power in the Aegean; but meanwhile, the Romans were defeating the Macedonians in a series of battles in the late third and early second centuries B.C.; by 146 B.C., Greece and the Aegean were essentially reduced to a Roman province. (The Ptolemies continued to rule in Egypt and Libya; but in 96 B.C. Ptolemy VII turned Cyrene over to the Romans; and by 30 B.C., Egypt was captured from the last of the Ptolemies - Cleopatra.)

The stepped road leading to the village.

Roman Santorini (146 B.C. - A.D. 395)

Little is known of Santorini under the Romans. They did take over the site of Ancient Thera, where they built their ubiquitous baths (p. 172) and reconditioned various other structures such as the theater (p. 172). Honorary and votive inscriptions at Ancient Thera refer to many of the well-known Emperors as benefactors - Tiberius, Trajan, Hadrian, Marcus Aurelius, Claudius, and others – but much of this was conventional flattery. Probably for most of the indigenous Santorinians, little or nothing changed; certainly neither Ancient Thera nor the island as a whole figured much in Rome's imperial calculations. And when Rome's power in this part of the world declined, Santorini ceased to maintain whatever urban culture it had known.

Byzantine Santorini (A.D. 395 - 1210)

With the division of the Roman Empire in 395 into Western and Eastern realms, Santorini became part of the latter, ruled from Byzantium, or Constantinople. Perhaps of more immediate significance, Christianity came to Santorini: according to an inscription in the old Basilica of St. Michael at Ancient Thera (p. 168), this occurred in the fourth century. Santorini seems not to have featured in affairs during the next several centuries, although in the eighth century it did join in the so-called "war of the icons", when Christians split over the question of whether they should portray the features of Christ and other sacred personages in painting and other mediums. As the Byzantine authority declined, the Aegean – indeed, most of the Mediterranean – became prey to pirates and marauders of various origins – Goths, Slavs, Saracens. Christianity must have provided some solace to inhabitants of remote islands such as Santorini, but there was no recognized power to advance their worldly estate.

Santorini under the Venetians (1210 - 1537)

In the end, that power was provided by a group of men who were, despite all their pretensions – and titles – little more than warlords (not to say gangsters). These were the Europeans who, in the name of the Fourth Crusade, ransacked Constantinople and divided up the Byzantine Empire in 1204. Since the ring-leaders happened to be from France, the new rulers of Greece became known in general as "Franks", but many parts were in fact "assigned" or "sold" to Italians. Indeed, it was a Venetian, Marco

Sanudo, who took over the Aegean islands as his share of the loot, setting up his capital on Naxos. In 1210, Sanudo broke with Venice and took an oath of fealty to the Holy Roman Emperor, Henry of Flanders; Sanudo was made the feudal superior of all the Aegean islands, including Santorini, and he assumed the grand title of Duke of the Archipelago and Sovereign of the Dodecanese. That same year, he gave one of his companions, also a Venetian, Barozzi, the island of Santorini as a fief.

This Barozzi moved in with some of his men and at least established the stability of such conquerors. He was succeded bys his son Andrew I in 1244, but in 1269 the Byzantine Greeks managed to reconquer Santorini along with many of the other Aegean islands. In 1296, however, the Venetians defeated the Byzantines, and Jacobo II Barozzi took over the rule of Santorini while the Sanudo family took back their Dukedom. In 1308, Andrew II assumed the rule of Santorini, and he was succeeded in 1334 by Marinos I. But the Sanudo family had long been feuding with the Barozzi family; in 1335, Nicholas Sanudo, Duke of Naxos, dethroned Marinos I and placed Santorini under the direct rule of the Sanudos and the Duchy of Naxos. Meanwhile, the Venetians had been building a number of castle-fortresses on Santorini at such places as Oia, Pyrgos, Emporion, Akrotirion, and Skaros. This last-named was a rocky pinnacle just north of modern Fira (p. 188), and this castle served as "capital" of Santorini during these years.

In 1383, the ruler of the island of Milos, Francesco Crispi, a Lombard nobleman, assassinated Nicholas II Sanudo and proclaimed himself Duke of Naxos. For the people of Santorini, this meant little difference. After Francesco's death, his son Jacopo assumed rule over Santorini and Naxos while other sons divided up the Cyclades. This led to a long series of rulers of the Crispi family – and considerable feuding within the family itself. The Turks meanwhile were becoming more and more of a power in this part of the world, and with the fall of Constantinople in 1453, the Crispi recognized that they now ruled essentially under the aegis of the Turks – and even paid tribute to the Sultan. The Venetians, however, could not accept this situation and they proceeded to fight a war with the Turks in 1463; Santorini, although it tried to remain neutral, ended by suffering at the hands of the Turks, so that when the peace treaty was signed in 1479, Santorini's population was down to a few hundred.

In 1480, Jacopo III Crispi married his daughter Fiorenza to the Venetian noble, Domenico Pisani, son of the Duke of Candia (Crete), which itself had been under Venetian rule since 1204. Santorini was part of the dowry, and this Pisani tried to provide a decent rule for Santorini. But when his

father-in-law, Jacopo III Crispi, died, his wife's uncle, Giovanni III Crispi, then Duke of Naxos, took Santorini back under the Crispi rule (even driving away the Venetian fleet that came to aid Pisani). When Giovanni III's son, Francesco, murdered his wife and almost murdered his son, Venice did intercede and exiled him to Santorini (and later to Crete). The Crispi family, however, remained in control of the Duchy of Naxos, including Santorini.

Santorini under the Turks (1537 - 1832)

Then, in 1537, the pirate chieftain, Khair Eddin Barbarossa (one of two Greek brothers from Mytilene who operated for the Turks) was terrorizing the whole of the eastern Mediterranean; he captured Santorini and essentially turned it over to the ruler of the Ottoman Empire, Sultan Selim II (known to the Western world as Suleiman the Magnificent). The Sultan, however, allowed the Duke of Naxos, Giovanni IV Crispi, to continue nominal rule over Santorini, but the last of the Crispi was outsted in 1566 and the Turks assumed direct rule of Santorini along with most of the other Aegean islands.

What saved Santorini during the following decades under the Turks – when so many parts of Greece suffered so terribly – was its relative smallness, isolation, and poverty. In fact, the Turks really didn't occupy Santorini; they established the taxes and tribute due, and then pretty much left the Greeks and "Franks" to their own devices – a kind of international protection racket. Yet these must have been difficult years for any people living there: they were, if not prisoners of the Turks, exiles from Greece. What is remarkable is that any sense of Greek identity survived. For one thing, the Venetian - Catholic element had long ago strongly implanted itself on the island, establishing churches, monasteries, and schools as well as dominating the political, social, and economic life of the island. Yet alongside this, the Greek-Orthodox element prevailed, establishing its own churches and schools, and keeping the Greek language and popular culture alive. Only once did the Santorinians receive encouragement from the world outside: in 1770, the Russians – both as fellow Orthodox and as enemies of the Turks – decided to assist the Greeks in rising up against the Turks; they annexed eighteen of the Cyclades, including Santorini, but it was in name only, and by 1774 they abandoned them to the Turks again.

Union with Greece 1832 to present

Then, in 1821, when the Greeks rose up on the mainland to declare their independence, one of the leaders of the revolution, Demetrios Ypsilantis, sent an envoy, Evangelos Mazarakis, to rouse the people of Santorini against the Turks. The Santorinians, however, were not in a position to take an especially active role in the struggle – partly due to their isolation, and partly due to the rivalry between the Orthodox and the Catholic elements on the island. But with the formal recognition of Greece's independence in 1832, Santorini joined the new Greek nation.

During the nineteenth century, Santorinians had some time to re-establish their sense of Greekness, but their trials were not over. In World War II, the Italians occupied Santorini in 1941; and when the Italians dropped out of the war, the Germans took over and remained in control until October 18, 1944. In the years since, the island has been allowed to develop, the main interruption being the great earthquake of 1956. But even that did not deter the Santorinians – although the population has been slowly shrinking, as part of a general pattern of retreat from rural societies and remote islands. Tourism and archaeology have combined since the late 1960s to bring a new prosperity and a new urgency to the island, but behind all the activity lies the unspoken: nature could easily undo man's handiwork on Santorini.

*The church of Ag. Minas
at Kato Fira.*

Visiting Santorini

When To Visit

The Best Season: Most visitors to Santorini come in mid-summer --June, July, and August; increasing numbers now come in May or September; other now come in April or October. Depending on your own schedule and tastes, you may well want to "buck the tide". During the high season, all the means of transport to and from the island, its hotels and cafes and restaurants, and its several popular beaches can be truly crowded; Fira can be turned into a shoppers' spree when a couple of cruise ships have disgorged hundreds of passengers there; the Akrotiri excavations can be a slow-moving line, public transportation can look like Cairo's, and restaurant menus gradually "collapse" as the dining hours wear on.

There are various ways of working around all this, of course-- dining at off-peak hours, seeking out less popular beaches, taking taxis, reserving seats on airplanes or staterooms on ships *well* in advance. But one thing that you cannot work around during the high season are overnight accommodations (see pp. 90 for details): there is simply a limit to how many beds can be produced on a given night. The young and the rugged always seem to find some bit of ground on which to stretch out their sleeping bags, but if you want the better hotels during the high season you must make your reservations well in advance. Work through an experienced travel agent or call or write on your own, but especially in July and August, make your travel plans for Santorini in advance. Or consider coming in June or early September or even late May: the weather is more than warm enough and there are enough "fellow travelers" to make it interesting.

But let it be said: one way or another, everyone gets fed and bedded down on Santorini. So come, and make your own way on Santorini.

C. MAVROPETRA

C. KOULOUMBOS

OIA
FOINIKIA
ARMENI
AYIOS NIKOLAOS
PANAGIA KALOU

C. RIVA
C. TINO
C. MUSAKI

THIRASIA

POTAMOS
C. SAMANDIRI
MANOLAS
AGRILIA

C. SKAROS
VOURVOULOS
MEROVIGLI
ST. NIKOLAOS
PHIROSTEFANI
ANO FIRA
SKALA FIRA
FIRA
C. KIMINA
KATO FIRA
C. TRIPITA
KARTERADOS
MIKRA KAIMENI
MANOLITHOS
NEA KAIMENI
DAFNI

PALEA KAIMENI
MESSARIA

VOTHON
ASPRONISI
EXOGONIA
ATHINOS
PYRGOS
EPISCOPI

MEGALO KHORION
PROFITIS ELIAS
KAMARI

C. AKROTIRI
AKROTIRI
ANCIENT THERA
AYIOS NIKOLAOS

MAVRO RAHIDI
EMPORION
PERISSA

EXOMYTI

SANTORINI

69

The weather

As for the weather, it follows the general patterns of the Greek-Aegean world, with the hottest period coinciding with the months of the high season - June, July and August. There is no denying that it can be unbearably hot during tht mid-day during those months: in that respect, May and September can be more comfortable for traveling about - although you then lose on the water temperature if swimming is your aim.

One special factor on Santorini is the wind (p. 36). Throughout the year, even during the hottest months – and especially with the *meltemi* of August – Santorini is a windy island, sitting out there as it does, on the edge of the Aegean, and with its exposed slope. But it is one of the elements that make Santorini such a fresh, invigorating place to visit, so you might as well enjoy it.

Just to give some objective standard, here are the mean (average) temperatures (for the 24-hour day) of the months on Santorini:

	C	F
January	11	51
February	11.1	52
March	12.2	54
April	14.9	59
May	18.7	66
June	22.7	73
July	25.1	77
August	24.6	76
September	21.9	71
October	19.1	67
November	16	61
December	12.9	55

Length of visit

How long you stay on Santorini will depend on a combination of your own desires and the available transportation. The quickest visits are those of the people who come ashore from the cruise ships that put into the harbor below Fira (p. 101); they usually have only a few hours, but for many people, the view of the island is, in fact, enough: the dramatic cliffs as the cruise ship pulls into the volcano's caldera is, in a sense, worth the price, while the donkey ride up to Fira and browsing through the shops are a dividend.

Another quick visit can be made by those who come down from Piraeus on the through-boat to Crete; they spend the time it takes this ship to go on the Crete, turn around, and then come back enroute to Mykonos or other points north – this has usually allowed only about 14 hours on Santorini. Now, though, there are Olympic flights linking Santorini to Crete and Mykonos (p. 75); utilizing this service for even one way would add to the amount of time available on Santorini in proportion to travel time. But even here, much depends on what you want to do with your time on Santorini: your hours on the island might turn out to be those when sites, museums and beaches are not accessible.

Cactas crowd the church.

The fact is that most visitors to Santorini depend on the ship connections with Piraeus (Athens) and Crete-Rhodes (pp. 78) – the former, of course, allowing for stopovers at other islands. (The Olympic flights, aside from being expensive, tend to be all booked up well in advance). An individual traveling the Greeks islands and committed to a rigid schedule and itinerary may find limited choices, but most people, with a little planning and lots of flexibility, can arrange to stay on Santorini about as long as it appeals to them.

How long that will be, of course, depends on individual interests and tastes. If you are looking for a spectacular panorama, an unusual atmosphere, and a few lazy hours on a beach, then 24 hours on Santorini may suffice. If you are the kind who likes to make maximum use of every moment, the fact is that you can take in the major attractions plus enjoy the occasional swim in about two days. However, you can just as easily fill three of four days with various excursions.

Suggestions as to how best to use your time on Santorini follow, but to put it into general terms for the average tourist, Santorini is a place that can be "done" in two or three days. As for moving about during this time, many people now rent the mopeds, motorbikes, and other such vehicles (p.) but these will not appeal to everyone; meanwhile, the public buses are apt to be woefully overcrowded during the peak season; since taxi fares are relatively cheap, the suggested schedule that follows is based on using taxis.

Using your time on Santorini

What follows is merely a suggested way of using your blocks of time on Santorini. Each "block" is a morning or afternoon of 3-to-4 hours duration. It is assumed you will be based in Fira, but this hardly matters since distances are so short (and if you are willing to take taxis). It also assumes that you will "do" the town of Fira in those odd hours between and around your other excursions: serious museum visitors however, will probably want to save one "block" for the Fira museums and exhibits. In any case, if you are planning a tight schedule, check all the hours of sites and museums (p. 115-127).

Block 1

Take taxi to Akrotiri site (p. 136) – enroute, stop at ancient church of Ayios Nikolaos Marmarinos (p. 154) – visit site of Akrotiri (with possible swim) – taxi over to Perissa (p. 153) (alternative swimming possibility) – taxi on via Pyrgos to Monastery of Profitis Elias (p. 176), with its vista and museum.

Block 2

Take bus (or taxi) to Kamari Beach (p. 154) – enroute, stop at Byzantine Church of Panayia Episkopi (p. 155) – walk (or taxi) up to site of Ancient Thera (p. 163) – walk (or taxi) down to Kamari Beach for a swim and / or refreshments.

Pyrgos from below.

Church in Pyrgos.

Panayia Episkopi.

Ayios Nikolaos Marmaritis.

Block 3

A boat excursion to the Burnt Isles (Kaimeni) and Thirasia: described on pages (181-186). But note that this is only feasible if you're on Santorini when such excursions are scheduled: this is at least once daily during the summer season. You can hire a boat to take you as in individual or with a small party, but it will be correspondingly expensive.

Block 4

Take taxi to Oia, stopping at as many of the monasteries, churches, caves, villages and other places enroute as interest you: this excursion is described on pages 186-190. Since this need not consume a full block of time, you could consider keeping the taxi to take you to several other sights on the island: Monolithos, for instance (p. 154), or the pumice quarry (p. 38), or some of the lesser known churches, if your interest happens to be Byzantine culture.

Traveling To and Around Santorini

It is assumed that the visitor is already on Greek territory before coming on to Santorini; in fact, the only way to get to Santorini directly from foreign territory is with one of the cruise ships (see below).

Air Since the early 1980s, Olympic Airways has been offering flights (in smaller aircraft) between Santorini and Athens and Santorini and Crete. (Crete, then, is linked by Olympic to Rhodes and Mykonos as well as to Athens). This air service to Santorini is available only during the main season; it is relatively expnsive; and it is reserved well in advance. But considering that it cuts the 14-hour trip by ship between Santorini and Piraeus down to about 1 hour (and the 6 hour or so trip between Crete down to even less than an hour), it should appeal to those with more money than time.

Cruise Ships Probably the largest single group of visitors to Santorini in high season are those who come ashore from the cruise ships that tie up in the deep waters below Fira. The passengers are taken off the cruise ships by small boats (all very safe--at most a bit of salt spray) and are put ashore at the little port of Fira; there people are now offered a choice of taking a donkey ride up the steps, riding the cable car, or walking (see below). Once up at Fira, many of the "cruisers" spend the brief time allotted in browsing, shopping, and eating in Fira. Depending on the time ashore, however,

Firastephani.

The wild beauty of Santorini.

Santorini near Emborion.

One of the many churches of the island.

some might decide to visit the local museum(s); and indeed, if someone had a special desire to visit the Akrotiri excavations or some other places on the island, a taxi would allow such an excursion even if the cruise ship did not offer a special tourbus. (Most now do.).

Cruise ships that include Santorini in their itinerary operate mostly out of Piraeus-Athens, but some originate in other Mediterranean ports (and occasionally even more distant lands). Some of these cruises are merely 2-3 days around several Greek islands; others are on more ambitious Aegean or Mediterranean itineraries; some are on still more far-ranging trips. All offer relatively fine accommodation at relatively fine prices. Not everyone cares for the cruise-ship life, but there is no denying that it is the easiest way for many people to at least sample a wide variety of what the Aegean offers. Inquire at any travel agent for the latest schedules, prices, and other details.

Scheduled Ships there are scheduled ships throughout the year connecting Santorini to Piraeus, at least some of the islands between there, and to Crete (and from there to other islands). During the main summer season, there are about two a day in both directions (that is, south to Crete or north to other islands and Piraeus). Some of the islands that these ships put into include: Ios, Naxos, Mykonos, Paros, Syros, Folegandros and Sikonos. Note that one of the ships to Crete connects to Ayios Nikolaos, Sitia (and then on to Rhodes via Kassos, Karpathos and Khalki) while another just goes to Iraklion. One way or another, then, Santorini can be easily incorporated in ship travels through the Aegean.

Because there are many changes in ship lines, schedules, fares, etc. from year to year, from summer to winter (and even from month to month), it would be misleading to try to provide too many details here—specific names of ships, times, fares, etc. In the end, furthermore, most people have to or want to travel on a particular day, so mnay of the options vanish. Because these ships can be so crowded—even "sold out"—during the peak summer weeks, the best advice is to go straight to a private travel agency, or the National Tourist Information office immediately upon arriving in Athens, Crete, or whatever island you intend to use as your jumping-off point for Santorini—and make your plans, including purchasing your ticket. Likewise, the first thing you should do upon arriving on Santorini is to purchase your ticket to leave! In high season, that is—and especially if you are traveling on a rigid schedule. Obviously, you will get a ship there and away, but if you leave your ticket purchase till too late, it may not be at the most convenient times.

Speaking of convenient times—these ships often leave off and pick up passengers at Santorini at less-than-convenient hours of the night or day (due to the fact that Santorini is merely one stop on a longer route). You must simply accept this as part of the adventure of traveling the Aegean. Also, heavy weather may occasionally interfere with the schedules — so that you find yourself waiting dockside for a couple of extra hours. Again, it goes with the territory.

All these ships offer a choice of several classes— from First Class (with private cabins and full dining facilities) to Deck Class (which includes a comfortable lounge chair in an enclosed area— if you lay claim to it early enough— and at least the possibility of snacks). Considering the length of the trip between Santorini and Crete (5-6 hours), most people settle for the cheapest fare; but the trip to and from Piraeus can last a solid 8-14 hours, depending on the number of stops enroute; you may well decide to spend the extra money on better accommodations. (Consider, too, that if you take the overnight ship back to Piraeus, you have saved a night's hotel cost— so a first class cabin may not be all that expensive).

Finally, most people look forward to arriving at the port of Fira, with its dramatic stairs snaking up the cliff-face and the attendant donkey-ride. In fact, the regularly scheduled island ships now leave off and pick up their passengers at the little port just south of Fira, Athinos (p. 101). (There are also some ships that leave off and / or pick up passengers below Oia: p. 186) Aside from missing the chance to take the donkey ride, you must now get from Athinos (or Oia) to wherever it is on the island that you are heading. Public buses meet all ships and take passengers to Fira, and there are always taxis that will take you anywhere on the island.

Mules vs. Cablecar We have been referring to the "donkey ride" to Fira, but in fact people are now offered mules or horses. And since the early 1980s., they must compete with a cablecar for trade. The cablecar is of Swiss make (and thus is sometimes known as "the teleferique") and was installed as a sort of gift by the wealthy Santorinian-Greek shipowner Nomikos. The muleteers feared they would be driven out of business, or at least lose a lot of money, so a percentage of all the cablecar fares goes to the muleteers— who argue, reasonably, that they still remain as the image of Santorini that draws visitors there. The fact is, the mules and horses could not handle all the increased traffic of recent years— especially when a couple of cruise ships are in port. So why not consider taking the mule / horse one way and the cablecar the other way. (The terminal for the cablecar is indicated on the town plan, p. 192). The cost for the cablecar and the mule is about the same. Of course you can always walk one or both ways along the stairs— although you should be warned that these are covered with (mostly) dried and powdery animal droppings that give off a decided odor. Considering how most people are atop such an animal for the first time in their lives, it's a surprisingly rigorous, bumpy ride; on the other hand, since so many people of all ages (and shapes) make it up and down, year-in and year-out, it can't be that difficult. The muleteers stay beside you all the way and, despite all the apparent slipping and weaving, are in control. The basic rule is simple: hang on!! (And hire an extra mule if you happen to have a lot of luggage).

Public Bases There is now quite frequent and reliable bus service between Fira and all the points of interest to visitors— at least in the peak season it is frequent. But it must also be said that during peak season many of these buses can be filled to ovreflowing: with all the luggage piled on the top and the young people jammed within, you would think you're in some Third World metropolis. The best you can do during high season is to try to travel "off-hours"— whatever these may be— or at least get to the bus stop early and be prepared to assert yourself. (Warning: there is little or no organization at the main bus terminal in Fira — Town Plan 5 — so you must simply push your way through). You may be able to pick up some of the buses along their routes if you interrupted your trip or have made a sidetrip, but try to get to a bus-stop: an already-crowded bus is not going to stop along the road.

To conclude, you will use the buses if you have the time and energy to make your way on to them; certainly they are a cheap way to get around. But if you are in any kind of a restricted schedule and are determined to make the most of your stay, a taxi or motorbike might be preferable means of transport.

Taxis: Taxis are used frequently by everyone on Santorini as throughout Greece: when the mass of people cannot afford vehicles, it is still cheaper to spend the occasional fare for a taxi. Since most people will be based in Fira, you will want to know about the main taxi stand: (6) on the Town Plan. You can usually count on picking up a taxi at other villages or beaches or even along the roads.

Taxi fares in Greece are subject to government control, and your driver should be able to produce a schedule of fares (in English); the rates, of course, are subject to normal inflationary pressures, but what you should know about are a few of the factors. A small fee is charged as soon as the taxi gets underway; then it is metered at so much per kilometer; if you take a taxi out of town and dismiss it, the rate is more than if you use the same taxi for the round trip; if you ask the taxi to wait while you visit a site or whatever, the driver is allowed to charge a (relatively modest) fee per hour of waiting time (to be calculated from 15 minutes after arrival); there is a

Harvesting.

Episkopi.

surcharge for after midnight; and the driver can charge a slight fee for each piece of larger luggage.

What taxis are not supposed to do is to charge extra for extra passengers, and this suggest a possibility for at least some visitors to Santorini. It is a common occurrence to arrive on a ship with a number of other travelers with whom you have a sort of "glancing" acquaintance; you then all go up to Fira and book your rooms, and if you do not find yourself bedded down next door to one another, you probably find yourself eating dinner next to one another in some restaurant. The next day you go off and hire a taxi to, say, Akrotiri – only to discover when you arrive there that all your fellow "glancers" have done the same. Not everyone will care to, but some might consider asking some of these fellow travelers if they want to share a taxi before setting off on such excursions.

What is usually done in hiring a taxi for a longish excursion, whether by a single party or a group of people, is to go to the driver and explain what it is you want to see; have an estimate of how long you expect to stay at particular places (i.e. an hour to walk through Akrotiri); then get the driver to quote you a fixed price for the total excursion. If you took one of the "blocks" (p. 72-75) as a 4-hour excursion, you might have to pay at least Dr. 2000. But considering that it would be almost impossible to visit so many places in such a brief time by any other means, and especially if two, three, or four people might be splitting the cost, the taxi fare becomes most reasonable.

Private Vehicles Only in the mid-1980s did it become possible to rent (hire) a car on Santorini, but there are not that many available at any one time (and arrangements should probably be made in advance). As for bringing your own car over to Santorini, this would involve special arrangements— for one thing, the regularly scheduled passenger ships cannot transport cars or unload them. So this is not really an option for most visitors. But the island is so small, and there are the other possibilities for getting around— buses, taxis, mopeds, etc -- so a car is not really missed. Again, though, if a private car is your preferred way of getting around, make some arrangement with a taxi driver to chauffer you around.

Chartered Buses Several tourist agencies operate tour buses to the major sites around the island, and for many people this is a preferred way of touring. Look into this when you arrive on Santorini.

Motorscooters, Mopeds, Motorbikes, Bicycles Motorized two-wheelers of one kind or another have virtually inundated Santorini. Most of the rental shops are in Fira; the vehicles get such rough wear during the high season that they can often have mechanical failures (but replacements are easily

The beach of Kamares.

provided); all in all, it seems a delightful way to see Santorini -- relatively cheap, complete flexibility, and nothing can beat the sheer exhileration of riding along the roads of this extraordinary island on a totally exposed two-wheeler. But be careful before you get carried away or ride off the edge of the volcano: there are usually no shoulders to the narrow roads, they can become slippery with dust and sand, and the trucks and buses and cars give little ground to the totally vulnerable two-wheelers. (Old-fashioned bicycles are actually harder to come by than the motorized varieties). Just go slow and take no chances and you should be able to "do" Santorini in this enviable way.

Boats During the summer season, at least, there are many organized excursions by small boats to the "Burnt Isles" and Thirasia (described on pages 181-186). There are also some small boats that take bathers to remote beaches over by Akrotiri. And anyone might try to hire a boat at the port of Fira or elsewhere: this kind of private excursion, of course, will be relatively expensive.

Hiking & Autostop (Hitchhiking) Distances are short enough on Santorini so that many people can and do walk between many of the points of interest: the overland route, in fact, will sometimes cut off a considerable amount of an already short distance between two points. A variation is to take a bus or taxi for one or another stretch of an excursion and walk the other stretches. Thus, you could take a bus to Pyrgos (p. 176) and walk up to the Monastery of Profitis Elias (p. 176); from there you could walk down across the "saddle" to the site of Ancient Thera (p. 159); after visiting this, walk down to Kamári (p. 154), from which point you deserve to take a taxi or a bus back to Fira. Several such combination trips are possible. As for hitchhiking, or autostop -- the relative scarcity of cars and trucks on the island cuts down greatly on your prospects of getting a ride, but the worse that can happen is that you might have to walk a few miles.

Touristic Facilities

Since practically all who visit Santorini center their activities (if not all their time) on the town of Fira, and since virtually all the facilities that concern visitors are in Fira, the following account of Santorini's touristic facilities combines those available on the island as a whole with those of Fira.

The famous stepped road to the capital.

Information and Assistance

From Off Santorini: Anyone wanting information about touristic matters on Santorini before arriving there has several possibilities: Greek Embassies, Consulates, and National Tourist Organization (EOT) offices in major cities around the world; private travel agancies (although beware: they often lack the latest information about schedules, rates, etc.); ship agencies, although only those that actually service Santorini will have any details.

Telephones and Telegrams: When telephoning Santorini from anywhere off the island, the prefix for all Santorini numbers is: 0286. In Fira, the phone company (OTE) (4 on the Town Plan) mantains an office that will assist in long distance calls and telegrams. Its hours during the summer season go from early in the morning till mid-evening, with a reduced schedule on Sundays and holidays: check in advance if you must make a call at a specific time. And warning: this office can be a madhouse during peak season -- long lines at each phone booth and all but unattainable connections to Athens and various other points. (In an emergency, send a telegram). One possible option: try to place your off-island call from a hotel (where, fairly or not, you can apparently be "jumped" to the head of the line in the phone office itself!).

Ship & Airplane Arrangements: Although this point has been made elsewhere, it cannot be stressed too much: during the peak months of summer, if you are travelling on a tight schedule you must make your reservations to and from Santorini as soon as reasonably possible. Olympic flights are usually booked well in advance, and even the ships can be sold out. Go at once to travel agents in Athens, Fira, or wherever and make your reservations.

Closing Days and Hours

Since many visitors to Santorini have a limited time to spend, it is especially crucial to know what hours are observed by the various facilities.

Holidays: Although as it happens, few of the major Greek holidays fall in the months when most visitors are on Santorini, it is still good to know about these closing days of most facilities. They are listed in the Practical Information A to Z ("Holidays").

Archaeological Sites and Museums: The hours for the individual ones on Santorini are given under their respective listings. But it must be repated: these hours are subject to change -- from year to year, season to season,

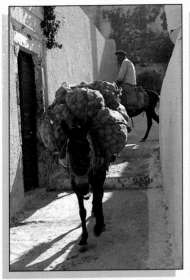

Carrying oranges...

grapes...

crates...

time for a break.

Fira: Skala to port.

Shopping in Fira.

Grape Harvest.

even month to month. Due to labor costs, in recent years the sites and museums of all Greece have been keeping increasingly restricted hours. So if these are your prime goals on Santorini, inquire immediately upon arrival as to the hours of particular sites or museums.

Shop Hours: See "Hours" under Practical Information A to Z. Be warned, though, that these, too, are likely to change from year to year.

Official Services

Passports, Customs, Currency: Since Santorini is part of Greece, and since it may be assumed that everyone who gets to Santorini will already be familiar with regulations governing such matters, it is enough to say that everything that applies to Greece applies to Santorini. See "Customs Control", "Money", and "Passports" under Practical Information A to Z.

Reductions and Passes: See this listing under Practical Information A to Z.

Postal Services: Stamps may be purchased and mail posted at the main towns and villages throughout the island, but most people will rely on the post office in Fira: 3 on Town Plan. Check its posted hours when you arrive.

Banks: There are two banks located side-by-side in Fira (8 on Town Plan); the National Bank of Greece is the one best organized to handle foreigners' transactions. Check the hours.

Water: The water situation has been discussed elsewhere (p. 36) but the main point is to realize that the water you will drink is totally safe -- at worst, it may have a mildly unpleasant, brackish taste. In any case, you will usually end up ordering plastic-bottled water from springs elsewhere in Greece.

Health Facilities: Although there is no full hospital on Santorini, there is a Public Health Station: there are several doctors and at least one dentist; and there are several pharmacies with a normal selection of medications.

Shops and Services

Basic Supplies: Most of the basic needs of visitors can be satisfied in Fira; camera supplies; stationery; toiletries; hardware; barbers and hairdressers; jewelers (including watch repairs); basic clothing; etc.

Souvenirs & Gifts: The souvenir and gift shops of Santorini are concentrated in the center of Fira, where literally thousands of people – mostly from the cruise ships – converge day after day in the high season.

Many of the goods are neither locally made nor locally "rooted": they are the jewelry and other wares found all over the Greek world: shirts, hats, pottery, leather goods, woolens, cottons, metalwork, alabaster, etc. Some of it is nice enough; in any case, it's a matter of taste. If you are persistent and seek out goods made on Santorini, you might find some embroideries or textiles; those with more money to spend might find a locally woven rug. Some of the costume jewelry is actually quite novel. Best is just to buy what you like and can afford and not worry too much about its being indigenous to Santorini.

Overnight Accomodation

As we have observed elsewhere, Santorini has not yet been fully developed for tourism; but this also means that overnight accomodations can be scarce during the peak summer weeks. Depending on your requirements, you will have little choice during those weeks, but somehow everyone finds a bed for the night. But if it's "the best" of Santorini you want during this high season, you had better make reservations in advance.

The only true Class A hotel is in Fira, the Atlantis; at Kamari, however, there are the fine Belonia Villas (Class A) and the Sunshine Hotel (Class B). Fira has some perfectly fine Class C hotels – the Kavalari, Panorama, and Pelican are right in the center of town, while the Kallisti Thira is a short walk to the edge. There are then numerous other Class C and other hotels throughout the island – at beaches such as Akrotiri, Monolithos, Perissa – or at all the major towns (Pyrgos, Messaria, etc.) Close to but not right in the touristic bustle of Fira are the hotels of Firostefani (to the north) and Karterados (to the south). Altogether, there are about 1600 beds available in the various hotels, pensions, and rooms-to-rent on Santorini.

Traditional Homes: The complex of traditional houses at Oia, sponsored by the Greek National Tourist Organization, is described in some detail (p. 190). There are other similar traditional houses for rent in the village just nort of Fira, Merovigli (but these are operated by private interests). Families and small groups might prefer these to the hotels.

Youth Hostels: There have been youth hostels in Fira and Oia.

Camping: There has been at least one camping ground set aside on the edge of Kamari, but young people tend to camp out all over the island (and it seems to be generally overlooked, even though the Greek government officially bans such impromptu camping).

For further comments about hotels, see that topic under Practical Information A to Z.

Eating on Santorini

Until the late 1970s, there were rather limited choices when it came to dining in the restaurants of Santorini. Now, during the summer months at least, there are a number of restaurants in Fira that serve quite fine meals with considerable style and at least a pleasing ambience. Undoubtedly part of the pleasure come from sitting on the edge of the cliff and looking out across the caldera as the sun sinks in the West: not many restaurants any place in the world can top that for ambience! The menus tend to be the familiar Greek restaurant choices – Santorini itself does not produce that much food, let alone anything very special (although it is a shame that most restaurants do not try to offer at least a couple of the local specialties, the fava soup or *pseftokeftedes*, described below). But the restaurants do a good job with the standards, and with a glass of the local wine, you can feel you are eating a meal attainable nowhere else.

There are now decent restaurants in various locales around Santorini – from Oia to Akrotiri – and the usual tavernas everywhere. But the biggest selection of restaurants by far is in Fira. Try a different one each night, while you're at it. Several of the more elaborate do not, in fact, enjoy a view but sit several streets back into town, but they usually offer outdoor gardens or roofs. One hint, though: if you have the choice, try to get to the popular restaurants a bit earlier – or later – than the crowds who almost overwhelm the service during the peak hours of the peak weeks. Especially if you want a particular location. (They can run out of particular items on the menu, however, if you come too late.)

For further comments on Greek restaurants, see that topic under Practical Information A to Z.

Specialties: Santorini is known for its cherry tomatoes, pistachio nuts, capers, and the fava beans. These fava beans are like lentils and are used to make a delicious soup, served with some olive oil, lemon, onion and oregano; alas, as Santorini has become more chic, it's harder and harder to find this peasant dish around the island. Likewise the other specialty, *pseftokeftedes* (or "false meatballs"): this is a flour batter with finely chopped tomatoes, onions, green pepper, eggplant, parsley, basil, salt and pepper – and even a bit of fava: these are usually served as a *meze*, or snack. But don't expect to find these at most restaurants these days. Likewise some of the special sweets are found only on special occasions. At baptisms and weddings, for instance, you might be offered *koufeta*, a sticky confection of roasted almonds boiled in honey; at Easter there are *meletenia,* wafer-thin pastry filled with mizithra cheese, eggs, sugar, and mastic flavoring.

As for the local wines, there is the *visanto,* sweet, strong and red; the *nykteri,* white, dry; and *brousko,* amber-red, full-bodied. Try some of the local labels – such as Markazenis' Cava Atlantis or Santinos.

Cafes: In addition to the many restaurants and tavernas, there are no end of cafes scattered around Santorini; these offer coffee and tea (now hot or cold), various soft drinks, usually ice cream and often milkshakes, some pastries and desserts, and possibly a selection of snacks (*mezes*). Oh yes – and these cafes now usually offer fruit juices – usually from cans or bottles, but nevertheless refreshing. Water at cafes is now apt to be sold in the ubiquitous plastic bottles. Unless the cafe happens to be especially crowded, you are usually left alone to nurse your drink as long as you please.

Activities on Santorini

Swimming and Water Sports

Some few visitors may want to do a little fishing or snorkeling or climbing on Santorini, but most are content to lie on the beaches and take the occasional swim. The beaches of Santorini are unusual in that they are composed mostly of dark volcanic sand and pebbles. They can be extremely hot during the summer weeks, and although they are not now especially bothered by tar, most people now travel with beach mats (sold everywhere) to save their towels. One phenomenon that has now come to be fairly routine on many of the beaches of Greece is that a goodly percentage of women now go topless on the beaches. (Nude bathing is officially prohibited on Santorini's beaches, but those who are determined to go nude usually find some place off by themselves).

There are any number of small beaches along the eastern coast, but the ones that attract most visitors are listed below. Directions for getting to them and other details of interest are given on the appropriate pages (including below in parentheses); here we simply characterize the possibilities.

Kamari: This is extremely accessible – with several buses daily in high season – and is probably the most popular. There is waterskiing, sailsurfing, and paddleboating; complete eating and refreshments available; numerous hotels and rooms. (p. 153).

Perissa: Now a popular beach with the backpackers and campers, it offers waterskiing, surfsailing, and paddleboating; some restaurants and cafes; and a few Class D hotels. (p. 148).

Akrotiri: Just a couple hundred yuears down from the archaeological site is a beach with a quite decent hotel and the chance to get a basic meal or snacks. Boats will take you to a better beach just a bit further along the coast. (p. 138).

Monolithos: This has become more popular and accessible in recent years; it has only Class bungalows (but in any case is close to Fira) but has facilities for basic meals and snacks. (p. 154).

The black beach of Kamares.

Night Life on Santorini

There has been one cinema in Fira but few foreigners are on Santorini to see bad movies. There are now quite a few bars and discos in Fira that attract the young set. Most visitors, however, prefer to sit quietly in outdoor cafes or just take a walk under the stars.

Churches and Chapels

There are said to be at least 250 churches and chapels on Santorini and if none is greatly important, many are picturesque, several are interesting, and a few have special significance. The name all 250 would be to turn this guide into a specialized catalogue that is beyond the author's competency and most visitors' interest. The more important ones, however, are described in some detail, and various others are indicated by name and location. Those who have a particular interest in this aspect of Greek life are invited to go exploring on their own.

Festivals and Popular Traditions

Since most visitors will probably find themselves on Santorini for a limited time during midsummer, they will not have that many opportunities to seek out festivals or experience the local culture. There is, however, on July 20, the name day for St. Elias, a festival in his honor at the monastery named for him (p. 173). And on August 15, in celebration of the Assumption of the Virgin Mary – and a major holiday throughout Greece – there is a festival at a church named for this event, the Panayia Episkopi (p. 155). Also, about mid-August the whole island takes on something of a festive atmosphere – it's known as the *ventema* – as all hands pitch in to harvest the grapes on which the wine (and traditionally much of their livelihood) depends.

Another possibility is to come across a village wedding (usually on Sunday afternoons) where they still keep alive many of the old traditions: processions, music, a ritual with grapevine branches, the church ceremony itself, feasting, and dancing. At Santorini weddings, the traditional dance is the *ballos*; the *syrtos* and the *repati* are two other favorite dances on Santorini. Still another event of special interest is to come across the grain harvesting, where they thresh the grain by using beast-drawn sleds and winnow it by tossing it into the air.

One tradition that few foreigners will be aware of these days is the telling

Ayia Ireni - Fira.

Orthodox Cathedral.

95

Catholic Church.

Roman catholic Bell Tower.

Ayios Minas

Ayios Ioannis - Fira.

98

Agia Ireni - Fira.

of vampire stories. No one knows for sure why the people of this island in particular became so interested in vampires, but one theory is that due to the peculiar nature of volcanic soil the bodies of the dead did not disintegrate as elsewhere and so it gave rise to tales of people "coming back from the dead". Don't expect to discuss vampires with your waiter, however – he's probably from Athens!

International Santorini Music Festival

Organized by the well-known pianist Athena Capodistria, this festival has been going since 1979 – usually in late-August and early September; it presents concerts of classical music by small ensembles or individual recitalists. The concerts are given in the Estia Hall in Thira. If you are interested, inquire as soon as you arrive on the island.

Arriving at Santorini

Santorini is one of those places – like the Grand Canyon, say – that is a natural phenomenon in itself, and surely one of the more unique experiences still left in this world of "done-it-all" tourists is to sail into its caldera-bay. To spot the black volcanic islets lurking in the center, to look up for the first time at the awesome, multi-layered and polychrome precipices, to see the town of Fira perched along the ridge – its jaunty white structures such a contrast to the bleak terrain – to feel the very silence and transparency of the enveloping air – somehow it evokes those fantastic tales of islands where people disembark and strange and menacing events transpire.

Santorini, of course, does not really threaten anyone, but it is certainly an unusual place and if you come in the right spirit perhaps you will experience a bit of wonder.

Getting Oriented

It depends, of course, on whether you are arriving from the north or the south, and at day or night, and whether your ship is putting you ashore at Fira's port or at Athinios (just along the coast to the south). In any case, at some point when arriving or departing, you should have a chance to look up at Fira and get oriented. You can get your bearings by starting on the south end (your right) of town, dominated by the dome of the Orthodox Cathedral and, just to its right, the Hotel Atlantis; a bit below these and further right is the small dome of the little Ayios Menas chapel. The town then stretches on to the north – with the famed *skala*, or steps, joining it at about mid-section – until the town just trails out. The next structure of any consequence, after an open space, is the Convent of Ayios Nikolaos (p. 188)., with its fortlike walls and dome. Then comes the small settlement of Merovigli (p. 188) while below it, on a prominent peak, is the site of the Venetian fortress, Skaros (p. 188).

Athinios

If your ship puts in at Athinios, as most scheduled Greek island ships now do, there is nothing to hold you here (although some of the abandoned, crumbling structures are said to date from the Venetian-medieval period) longer than it takes you to get either the public bus or private taxi to Fira (although, of course, the taxi can take you to any destination you desire). And whatever your destination, you could share a taxi with some fellow travelers. There are numerous cafes at Athinios to help you pass the time while waiting for your ship.

Fira-Port

If you are put ashore at Fira's port – also by a small boat – there is a bit more to enjoy, with its straggle of houses, a few cafés, its chapel, and a sleepy port atmosphere. It also has a public toilet and some ship-line agents. And off to the north, perched on the edge of the volcanic cliff like some Hollywood set-designer's vision, is an impressive castle-fort. Some claim it dates back as far as the thirteenth century, but more likely the present structure is only 400 - 500 years old; even at that, it has undergone considerable renovation. It belonged to one of the aristocratic Italian families, the Delenda; fittingly enough, the Italian occupation forces used it in World War II.

To get up to Fira visitors now have three choices – the traditional mules/horses, the modern cable, and plain old-fashioned shanks' mare. The mules and horses are mounted at a special point just behind the two central cafes; the ride up takes about 15 minutes (while to walk up takes some 20-30 minutes, depending on an individual's stamina: and in the heat of midsummer, it can be quite taxing). You can hire an extra animal if yuou have large amounts of luggage. At the top you dismount at about Step 540 (they are numbered on the shallow rises) (7) on the Town Plan. From there you walk the remaining steps – passing by the first of many gift shops and

Approaching Fira.

Port of Fira.

Delenda Fort - Port of Fira.

Dinner in moonlight.

A nightview from the island.

View of Fira.

Skala Fira.

The picturesque capital.

eating places – until you come to Step 587 at the very edge of the town's crossroads. (Incidentally, the long stairway road, the Skala Fira, has been named in honor of Spyridon Marinatos, the achaeologist who, among other achievements, excavated the great site at Akrotiri).

The Town of Fira

With its permanent population of about 2,000, Fira hardly qualifies for more than an overgrown village, yet during the peak weeks of the summer tourist season it seems more like some cosmopolitan center. This is not necessarily a recommendation, especially to those who think they are going off to some "simple" island paradise. The sheer numbers of gift shops, jewelry stores, cafes, restaurants, bars and various other touristic enterprises have undeniably overwhelmed the indigenous character of the center of Fira, and everyone must decide for themselves how to react to and deal with this. If it truly bothers you, of course, you don't even have to go to Fira: your ship will most likely deposit you at Athinios from where you can take a taxi to some other destination on the island – and then spend your entire vacation seeing and enjoying all the rest of Santorini. This is quite easy to do these days.

But most visitors aren't as strong-willed or single-minded, so the best thing is to take Fira for what it has become. One way to "rise above" the crowds, of course, is to look around and pay attention to your surroundings – read about the history of the town and the island, then seek out the remainders of that history. This guide is admirably suited to enhancing this approach to Fira. As well as serving as the "capital" of the island, for instance, Fira is the seat of a Greek Orthodox Bishop and at least half a seat of a Roman Catholic Bishop: so it is that the two most impressive buildings in Fira remain the Metropolitan Cathedral (p. 111) and the Roman Catholic Church.

With its church domes and bell-towers, its arcades and buttresses, its steps and portals, the soft curves interacting with strict lines, Fira appears to be almost an abstract composition (and a photographers' and painters' paradise!). Sometime in your stay in Fira, however brief, you should make a point of taking a walk from one end of town to the other, exploring the narrow, hilly streets, poking in and out of alleys and courtyards. Particularly in the northern end of town – the medieval - Venetian section known as *ta phrangika* (Greek for "Frankish quarter": the Turks term for the same place was *frankomahala*) – you may be surprised at what you encounter – coats of arms, mosaic stonework on the streets, and various architectural fancies.

Perhaps an even more special experience is to take a walk at night to the edge of Fira – north or south. As the local people go to bed quite early, you will meet hardly anyone, and it becomes something like a deserted town; even with the wind blowing, trees creaking, loose doors squeaking, and your own footsteps on the cobblestones, it is the peculiar silence of the atmosphere that strikes you. Silence and lights: the stars above, Fira and the other towns spread out across the island, and far below, the harbor, buoys, and ships.

Fira's Touristic Attractions

Everything of interest to the visitor – information sources, police, ship schedules and other means of transportation, telephones, post office, banks, hotels, restaurants, etc. – has been dealt with under their respective headings on pages 86-92.

Fira's Attractions

The Orthodox Cathedral of the Panayia Ipapanti ("Our Lady of Candlemas") (13) on Town Plan.

This was erected to replace the cathedral destroyed in 1956; it was built under the aegis of the Metropolitan Gabrial of Santorini, with private donations and state funds. It is one of the largest and newest cathedrals in the Cyclades; it lacks, however, anything very old; its crystal chandelier is quite impressive.

It has been announced that starting in the late-1980s there will be open to public, in a building attached to the Cathedral, a small collection of ecclesiastical works: Byzantine icons, books and manuscripts, vestments, and liturgical objects. Inquire if you are interested in such things. (And note that there is one similar collection at the Monastery of Profitis Elias: pp. 181)

The Roman Catholic Church of the Immaculate Conception, (14) on Town Plan.

Sunday Mass: 9:30 a.m.

The Roman Catholic presence on Santorini dates from the Venetian occupation of the thirteenth century; at one point it was extremely prominent, with French as well as Italian priests and nuns staffing their

A view of Fira.

own network of churches, schools, monasteries, convents, and other institutions. Now, although there are some practicing Roman Catholics on Santorini, the Fathers and Sisters have declined to only a handful. There is a Roman Catholic Bishop, however, responsible for Syros and Santorini; he divides his time between the two islands, usually residing on Santorini during the summer months.

The large Roman Catholic "compound" - at the north end of town – dates from the nineteenth century, when the Catholics consolidated their shrinking forces. The Church of the Immaculate Conception is shared by the Lazarist priests and the Sisters of Charity, who run the Rug and Handicraft School (see below).

About a half-dozen Sisters of the Dominican Order use the small Church of the Blessed Mother of the Rosary.

Ayios Menas, (16) on the Town Plan.

This is the little Byzantine chapel so familiar from countless photographs and artists' renditions that it has become the symbol of Santorini. This Saint Menas was a relatively obscure third-century martyr in Egypt; he also happens to be the patron saint of Iraklion, Crete.

Ayios Ioannis Theologos, (15) on the Town Plan.

This church was built around 1650 – by which time, of course, the Turks ruled Santorini but were willing to let Greeks go their own way religiously, so long as they continued to pay their taxes.

The Corogna Ducal Mansion, (19) on Town Plan.

The Corogna family was one of the many Italian families that established themselves in the Aegean as a result of the Fourth Crusade (p. 60). The Corognas had been based on Sifnos, an island to the north of Santorini, since 1307; but in 1560 they moved down to Santorini; they built their "Ducal Mansion" here in 1590. Now it is in ruins, but you can still see their coat-of-arms with its crowned eagle

The Rug and Handicraft School, (24) on Town Plan.

This was founded under the patronage of the former Queen Frederika of Greece (mother of the deposed King Constantine) and is operated by the Roman Catholic Sisters of Charity. The school accepts young girls between the ages of 13 to 16, from poor families; the girls stay at the school for 2 to 3 years while they learn the craft of rugweaving (as well as various other handicrafts – embroidery, etc.). The large rugs they make are sold to help defray the expenses of the school, and it is something to hear and see the large looms all rattling away. A small selection of embroideries, woolen goods, etc. made by the girls and Sisters are also for sale.

At the end of their schooling, each girl receives a small loom and about 50 pounds of wool; they then continue their weaving at home; the looms they use can make rugs up to about 2 yards and 4 yards long.

The Museums of Fira

Bronze Age (Cycladic) Culture

(21) on Town Plan.

Note: As this museum was not yet completed at the time of publication, there was no available information about its hours, admission fee, etc.

Introduction

The finds from the Bronze Age sites of Santorini – principally from the Akrotiri site (pp. 138-148) – are in a state of flux. There have long been some on display in Fira's Museum of Historic Cultures (pp.127-129). The French School of Archaeology in Athens has a fine collection of Cycladic remains – principally ceramics – from the nineteenth-century French excavations at Akrotiri and other places on Santorini (pp. 138-139). (There are even some remains in the Geological and Palaeontological Museum in Athens.) Then, in 1971, a selection of the finest works found at the Akrotiri site since the excavations that began under Professor Marinatos in 1967 (pp. 141) went on a temporary special display at the National Archaeological Museum in Athens. About this same time, a new museum for the Akrotiri finds was announced for Fira, to be open in late-1980s. At the moment of publication, the museum was still not open and there was some uncertainty of the ultimate location of the temporary display in the Athens Archaeological Museum. Meanwhile, the years since 1971 have seen still more finds at Akrotiri: and to further complicate matters, it was not certain whether the contemporaneous finds from the other collections (mentioned above) would be brought to this new museum.

Faced with these several unresolved matters, this guide has attempted to do the best possible at this moment: to describe the most significant finds (at least up to the time of publication) from the Akrotiri site: this guide could then be used either at the Archaeological Museum in Athens or at the new museum in Fira.

View from Fira down to Caldera.

Old balcony Fira.

116

Doorway in Fira.

A beautiful bell-tower.

Traditional courtyard.

View south from Fira.

The Exhibits

The Frescoes

Only the major frescoes are described here; there are many smaller fragments on display; and more are expected, since many upper stories at Akrotiri seem to have had frescoed walls. These are true frescoes: that is, the pigments were painted on the wet plaster. The reason for the fine state of preservation of these Akrotiri frescoes is that they were covered in volcanic ash, which due to its chemical content does not destroy pigments as much as do ordinary earths.

"The Spring Fresco" (or "Lilies Fresco")

This is a most lovely and quite unique fresco depicting the springtime of nature in an almost abstract manner. It covered three walls of a room (the fourth was occupied by the door and window) some $7^1/_2$ feet by $8^1/_2$ feet; the room seems to have been some kind of sanctuary. The fresco was found almost intact; it was painted against a whitish background, with a top band across the wall painted red. There are three main motifs; the rocks, the birds, and the flowers.

The rocks are variously black, red, green, or yellow, and are of irregular shape – clearly volcanic in origin; some have what appears to be a green moss on them. The birds are swallows, flying about alone or in pairs; the pairs seem to be in mating flights. The artist attempted to portray them with perspective. Swallows, by the way, are no longer found on Santoniri, so this is a valuable glimpse into the pre-eruption world.

As for the flowers, they are lilies, but combining the characteristics of several species; and where the lily has six stamens, these have only three. But since the lilies are mostly depicted here in groups of three, presumably the artist was deliberately working with symmetry and/or symbolism. The triple lily, in fact, is familiar from Egyptian paintings and also from the frescoes found at a villa at Amnissos, Crete (p. 141). But even though the artist was working within certain conventions, he managed to infuse these flowers with a sense of naturalness, of responsiveness to the wind, of life.

"The Antelope Fresco"

This fresco was found in a room in Quarter B, a second-story room. Around the upper part of the room was a continuous wreath of ivy (which

Bell-tower baking in the sun.

has here been restored). On the north wall were depicted two animals with upright horns; a third, similar but headless, was on the east wall; two more were depicted on the west wall. The animals are a hybrid of gazelles and of the antelope known as the oryx (*Oryx Beissa*), distinguished by its longish, straight, sharp horn. It is now mainly found in East Africa, but it was more widely distributed in ancient times. The question is whether the oryx was living on Santorini or Crete, or whether it was simply a subject the artist knew from elsewhere. (This latter seems the more likely.) But whoever the artist, and however he came to know the subject, these animals are depicted with incredible vivacity and deftness. They have been done in a highly stylized manner, with an outline of alternating heavy and fine lines and only a few internal details. It is one of those works of art where the simple primitive attains the heights of total sophistication.

"The Boxing Boys Fresco"

On the south wall of this same room (with the antelopes) were depicted two youths – hardly more than boys – boxing. The one on the left wears what appears to be a black boxing glove – the first such known in history. This boy also wears more jewels (including a gold ring in his ear) and appears slightly older than the one on the right: undoubtedly there was some significance to all these details. Both boys have the long hair associated with many Minoan youths; underneath the dark locks can be seen a blue layer that denotes a shaved head. Quite aside from offering us a glimpse into some ritualistic episode, the painting impresses as one of the most charming works of this era.

"The Monkeys Fresco"

In another room in Quarter B, on two walls, were depicted seven or eight lifesize monkeys; they are climbing over volcanic rocks and seem to be pursued by dogs. They are painted blue – as were some monkeys in the House of Frescoes at the Palace of Knossos on Crete. These monkeys are believed to be the species *Cercopithecus callitrichus*. It is not certain whether these monkeys were ever to be seen on Santorini or Crete, but the odds are that if they were they had been imported for a kind of zoo. (A fossilized skull, possibly of a monkey, has been found on Santorini, but its significance is as yet unknown.) They were probably portrayed here for their associations with some religious belief.

"The African"

In a room in Quarter A were found fragments revealing the head of an African or Asiatic man: dark skinned, thick lips, pug nose, short hair – all mark him as someone apart from the Aegeans. He was also wearing feathers in his hair, and a large ear-ring: now, one of the boxers (see above) is wearing an ear-ring, but neither Minoan - Cretans nor Mycenaean - Greeks have ever been known to wear such rings. Does this say something about the ancestry of the Santorinians (see p. 49) for claims about their origins)? Or does it say something about their apparent pre-occupation with exotic subjects in their frescoes?

In this same room, by the way, were found other fragments depicting a shrine or altar, with floral columns and horns of consecration – typical Minoan motifs. Two monkeys were also depicted in what seems to be prayerful pose.

"The Frieze of the Expedition"

This most extraordinary fresco was discovered in 1972. It ran as a band, or frieze, along the upper area of three walls of a room on the third floor of what is known as the Western House. The dimensions of the room were about 12 feet by 13 feet, and out of the approximately 37 feet of the original frieze, about 21 feet have been recovered. The band was 16 inches high on two walls, and 8 inches on the other.

When first discovered, it was thought that it depicted scenes from everyday life on Santorini – peaceful fishermen, for instance, and sponge-divers. Gradually, as pieces were cleaned and fit together, Professor Marinatos came to decide it was in fact quite an unfamiliar subject: the narrative, or "mini-epic", depicting a punitive expedition in North Africa. (The sponge-divers are now thought to be the drowned bodies of the dead warriors.) As such, Marinatos considered it "the most valuable document... from the Bronze Age" because of its uniqueness as a narrative of an apparently real episode.

But in more recent years, a new interpretation has been set forth by none other than Professor Marinatos's daughter, Nanno, herself an archaeologist and expert in Theran art. Drawing on close study of the details of the Akrotiri frescoes and on her knowledge of their total context, she rejects the notion that this frieze depicts some actual naval expedition to Libya. She does believe that the section on the north wall (the higher band) depicts a naval victory of Aegeans (possibly Therans) over non-

Aegeans, but sees no need to locate it in Libya. And the longer south-wall frieze she sees as a marine festival, perhaps commemorating a military victory but in a ritualistic sense, not as some historical document. The room itself, she believes, was used for some religious ritual (as were most of the rooms with frescoes, she believes).

"Spring Festival Fresco"

This was found in 1973 in an isolated building of at least three floors; the fresco seems to have covered the four walls of a first-floor living room. Among the motifs are six small nymphs (note their pink fingernails) picking flowers and carrying them in baskets to a bare-breasted, life-size woman – evidently a goddess; she is attended by a peacock-like bird, and elsewhere are more of the monkeys that these people were so fond of. On the second floor of this building, by the way, was found a painted stucco relief in the form of a frame, with a background of rosettes – possibly the backing of a throne or bed.

Household Objects

"The Wooden Bed and Stool"

In the same room as that with the Lily Fresco (see above) were found a wooden bed and stool. Now, when it is said that wooden objects were found at Akrotiri (or most contemporaneous sites) what was in fact found were the *holes* where the wood (or similar perishable material) had been. Surrounded by the pumice or ash, the wood gradually disintegrated; reacting chemically with the surrounding matter, the wood essentially evaporated. Meanwhile, the surrounding matter formed a hard surface around the wood so that as the wood vanished, the hardened matter retained its shape around the hollow. Archaeologists learn to recognize when they have come across such a hole; it is filled with a kind of plaster that is carefully extracted when hard; the former object can then be reproduced by removing the plaster from its "mold".

The bed is a most impressive object, since its "mold" was virtually intact: even the imprints of the rope used for the cross - frame were found. (What was not found intact has been clearly replaced by a different material.) Note the bed's small size: it is about 2 ft. 3 in. wide, and only about 5 ft. 4 in. long – confirming other evidence that these early Aegeans were relatively short.

The stool was crushed, but enough survived to allow for a reconstruction. This basic type of stool is known from certain Cycladic marble statuettes portraying people sitting on stools.

Both the bed and the stool have been reproduced in olive wood by a modern Greek furniture-maker to show what the originals looked like.

"The Basket (or Hamper)"

This was found in the so-called Mill House in Quarter A. Excavators discovered it by spotting traces of some dark substance in an all-white ash; with the most painstaking clearing, and then hardening of the dark dust with the proper gluelike solutions, the basket was eventually removed and restored. It is elliptical, or egg-shaped, and probably once had handles; these did not survive, but similar baskets are used to this day in Greece. The basket was made of plant fiber.

"Metal Vessels, Tools, etc."

Quite a few metal objects have been found in various rooms at Akrotiri: bronze vessels, ewers, trays; knives, daggers (some bearing traces of the original wooden handles); chisels, sickles; scale-weights including a graduated set of lead weights; etc. Of particular interest is the bronze ewer with the schematized papyrus-lily motif hammered around its shoulder.

"Food-Preparation Utensils"

Many stone tools and gridstones were found; also many clay cooking utensils, strainers (with sieve bottoms), and mortars-and-pestles. Of particular interest are the roasting grills (*kateutes*, in Greek): These small clay supports have ridges, or grooves, along the top edge; these held the small spits on which the food was grilled.

Ceramics

There are too many vases and other ceramic objects found to be able to describe them all in detail here; furthermore, it is not yet known how they will be displayed in the new Fira museum. All we shall attempt to do here is to point out a few general characteristics and then single out several of the more unusual objects.

a) In general, the pottery from Akrotiri falls into two groups: the locally

Fira - Mosaic in courtyard.

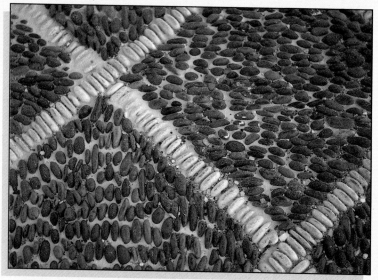

Cathedral, Pebble Mosaic.

Fira - Mosaic in courtyard.

made ware; and the imported wares from Crete, other Aegean islands, or the Greek mainland.

b) The pottery also might be grouped in another way: the domestic-functional; and the ceremonial-religious.

c) Along with the great variety of shapes, you will want to focus on the often simple yet ever lovely decorations. Natural motifs – lilies, reeds, crocuses, dolphins, etc. – were most common, and whether rendered realistically or stylized, it was always with a deft economy. We may assume, too, that many of the subjects had some symbolic value to these ancient people: thus a flower pot showing severed flowers falling to the ground depicts flowers with no stamens – the whole subject probably representing the death of nature.

"Offering Tables"

Two small tables, each with three legs, they are made of stucco rathern than clay. The rims of both are painted with a wavy red ornament. The legs of the higher of the two are painted with dolphins and marine flora. Such tables were common throughout the Minoan, Cycladic, and Mycenaean world; they were used either for offerings or incense-burning for the gods.

"The Bull Rhyton"

This clay object evidently represents the *Bos primigenus*, the original wild bull. It had large horns, but these are represented here as cut off – a practice that made the bulls less dangerous. Over its body is painted a red woolen net, indicating the bull was used in some sacred rite. (Similar bulls-in-nets were represented in Minoan works, and since they were mentioned in Plato's account they have been prominent in claims linking Santorini and Crete to Atlantis: p. 28). Santorini could hardly have supported a population of bulls for sacrificial rites; instead they sacrificed small clay figurines (several of which are also on display).

"Lion's Head Rhyton"

This superb piece seems to be imitating in clay some metal prototype.

"Inscribed Ewer" (No 1371)

This is particular value because on its shoulder is an inscription in Linear

A, the script known from Crete (and only a few other sites). It has been translated as "Aresana" – possibly the name of a person or place, possibly a pre-Hellenic goddess.

"The Grapes Ewer" (No. 623)

This is of interest as it is the earliest known representation of grapes.

The Museum of Historic Cultures

(22) on Town Plan.

Visiting Hours: As with all Greek museums, the days and hours for visiting seem to be in a state of flux. If you definitely want to see this collection, inquire immediately on arriving in Fira – and make your plans.

Entrance Fee: Drachmas 100 (but will probably go up).

Photographs: There has not been any guide to or picture-postcards of the collection, so some objects – but not the choice ones – can be photographed for a fee; inquire beforehand if you want to photograph particular objects.

Introduction

This museum is an outgrowth of the original collection of Friedrich Hiller von Gaertringen (1864 - 1947), the German responsible for the excavations at Ancient Thera between 1896 - 1903 (pp. 165-166). He started the collection in a building in Fira in 1902; this new museum opened in 1970. Most of the contents are from Ancient Thera, but some are from other sites, including various objects from the Cycladic era sites of Santorini; when the new museum of the Bronze Age culture opens (p. 115), presumably all such objects will be transferred there. This will then leave this museum as essentially a collection of works from about 800 B.C. into the early centuries of the Christian era: Geometric, Archaic, Classic, Hellenistic, Roman, and Byzantine periods. Although hardly a major collection, there are several fine pieces, and the whole is interesting for what it reveals of the remote, provincial world's cultural level.

The Collection

Reception Hall

Here have been displayed various ceramics found at several of the

Cycladic - Minoan era sites on Santorini (including Akrotiri and the pumice mines) by both the earlier German excavation of 1899 - 1900 (p.140) and the more recent Greek excavation. The large pithoi have been against the wall, the small wares in a display case.

Long Hall

You know step (opposite the reception desk) into a long hall; it might be thought of as three areas, and you move (to the left) to the end for the first section.

This first section includes urns and vases dated from 800 to 600 B.C. in the Geometric and Orientalizing styles common throughout much of the Aegean world at that time. Note especially, standing in the center of this area, a superb Archaic amphora from a cemetary of the seventh century B.C.: on the neck is relief decoration with a pelican, while on its shoulders are charioteers with Pegasus.

The second section includes amphorae of the Geometric - Cycladic style and much Proto - geometric pottery. Note especially, against the wall (just at the corner of the entrance) in a small glass case, a terra-cotta statuette of a woman, interpreted as representing a mourner. Dated to about 650 - 600 B.C., this is the so-called Daedalic style, which developed on Crete; it is a transitional form of sculpture that was breaking away from the rigidities of the Orientalizing style and pointing toward the more flexible Archaic art of the Hellenic world.

The third section of this hall includes many large amphorae from the Geometric cemetery at Ancient Thera. The Geometric vases found here are in a recognizable sub-style sometimes known as "Santorini vases."

Note in the center of this area an Archaic *kouros*, or youth, dated to about 650 B.C.

Rear Hall

You now step into the hall that is perpendicular to the long hall you have just walked through. Starting immediately to the left, and then working your way clockwise around the hall, you will note:

At the side: Vases from the Geometric cemetery; Corinthian and Ionian vases of the sixth century B.C. (Note that a new delicacy has appeared in the work).

Along rear wall: The Archaic lion from the agora of Ancient Thera (c. 600 B.C.); a case of Attic black-figured vases; a case of Attic red-figured vases;

and at the far corner, sculptured heads of Aphrodite and a youth.

Against the side wall: a grave table.

Wall beside entrace: portrait heads; a case with vases, including a fine Attic cup from the third century B.C.; and a case with vases from Archaic graves: note especially the inscribed bucchero vase, a covered dish, and small bronze unguetariums.

In cases in center of room: Attic black-figured vases; Attic "Little-Master" cups; and a collection of terra-cotta figurines from the Archaic cemetery (c. 650 - 600 B.C.): several are most fascinating – dolphins, monkeys, ducks, turtles, frogs; satyrs (including one with an erection and riding a horse) and a wizened old man with prominent genitals.

Sculpture Lobby

Retracing your way back to the reception hall, you proceed through it into a small room on its other side; here are sculptures from the Hellenistic and Roman periods at Ancient Thera. Among the more notable pieces are: a statuette of Aphrodite fastening her sandal; Roman reliefs of centaurs and lapiths; and a portrait bust (first on right, as you enter the lobby), from the Royal Portico at Ancient Thera: it is exceedingly elegant.

Courtyard

Off this room, through a glass door is a courtyard with a collection of sculpture and stonework from Ancient Thera. (Ask the person on duty at the reception desk to admit you if the door is locked). Included among the more interesting pieces are: some fine sculptured heads and gravestones; a column inscribed with a letter by Ptolemy VI Philometer; an inscribed lingam (phallus); a bull's head; a grimacing mouth; a bench with an elegant relief carving; and in the center of the courtyard, a large columnar table with garlands and bulls' heads in relief.

Basement

Here are some glassware, and various other artifacts from the late Roman and the early Christian periods.

Ghyzis Palace (Megaron Ghyzis)

(23) on Town Plan.

Visiting Hours: Daily except holidays: 10:30 - 1:30, 5:00 - 8:00.

Entrance Fee: 100 Drachmas.

This is the newest member of Santorini's cultural family. It is housed in a completely restored 17th century "palace" or mansion that once belonged to the Ghyzis family; the local Roman Catholic Church, which owns the property, paid for the work with the idea of making it a cultural center. Meanwhile, Dimitris Tsitouras, a well-known Athens lawyer and art collector, had been nurturing a dream of setting up a museum. After he became so drawn to Santorini that he bought a house here in the mid-1970s, he saw his chance and went to work to build up a collection of maps, landscape drawing, costume engravings, depictions of all the daily life, and any other aspect of Santorini between the 15th and 19th centuries. Each work on display is fully indetified. There are also some paintings by 20th

Ghyzis Palace Museum.

century Greek artists such as Spyros Vassiliou and Yiannis Morals – again, with Santorini as their subject. Tsitouras is also building up an archive and library of documents and printed texts of all kinds relating to the history of Santorini. (Access to this is for now limited to those who can establish scholarly credentials).

All in all, a most delightful addition to Santorini's life – and a counterweight, if not an antidote, to the many discos that have sprung up. Step inside this lovely small museum – it will reward even a short visit.

Excursions

For all the excursions on Santorini described in the following pages – although the bus routes are used as the basic structure – the detailed accounts are written as though everyone has independent means of transportation, whether taxi, moped, private car, or whatever. Put another way: the bus schedules are relatively limited (and the buses often so crowded) that many a visitor, with a restricted schedule, would not be able to make any of the little stops and sidetrips. Therefore, the description of all such places enroute to the main destination assumes you are able to break the journey.

Akrotiri

This is the site that has been gaining so much publicity for Santorini since its unearthing began in 1967; it may or may not have anything to do with "lost Atlantis" (pp. 24-30), but it has certainly revived that debate. The finds should be on display in the new museum in Fira especially constructed for them (p. 115). The site itself is not all that spectacular – compared, say, to Knossos or Pompeii – yet it is emerging as a major site and is interesting for the glimpse it provides of such a site being discovered: it is a bit like being with Schliemann at Troy, or Evans during his first years at Knossos. The season's digging usually occurs during the mid-summer weeks. Even if you do not have a special interest in archaeology, it can be a worthwhile excursion, especially as it can be combined with various other side-trips.

Visiting Hours: During peak season at least, open almost every day 8:00 - 7:00 (but check before going off to see it).

Entrance Fee: Drachmas 150.

Photographs: There has been no fee and no restrictions for hand-held cameras.

Abandoned old windmill near Akrotiri.

View of island from Akrotiri road.

Athinos - port.

Akrotiri - North court.

Akrotiri - Overview of site.

How to get there:

Buses: There are both private tour buses (see various travel agencies around Fira) and public buses to Fira. If you have more time at the site than you need for examining the remains, make your way down to the beach (see below) where there are modest meals available. (There is a small C Class hotel at Akrotiri, too, if you wanted to stay overnight).

Taxis: Those with limited time on Santorini might prefer to take a taxi – especially if you are a party of 3-4. A quick ride there, a reasonably brisk walk through the site while the driver waits, and the return to Fira can be accomplished in the two hours; it could be combined with stops at several other places for a full "block" (see pp. 72-73).

Hiking: The Akrotiri site is about as far removed from Fira as anyplace on Santorini, but a hike might be combined with a ride to some other point.

The Trip to Akrotiri

Leave Fira by C (Town Plan: A-9), the main road to all points south. (There is an old dirt road that cuts directly south from the end of Fira (past the Kallisti Thira Hotel: 29 on Town Plan), but this will not entice many people.)

2 Km.: Pass a turn-off (to left) to the village of Karterados; this village was once famed throughout the Mediterranean for its far-flung mariners; its menfolk now tend to farm or work in commerce.

3 Km.: Pass a turn-off (to right) that leads up to the village of Messaria. Just opposite this, a turn-off (to left) leads over to Monolithos (p. 154) or on to Kamari (p. 159).

4 Km.: Proceed on past the village of Vothon (on left) and begin the climb up toward Pyrgos. (Vothon has one church built inside a cave).

6 Km.: The old dirt road from Fira joins the main road at this point.

7 Km.: A turn-off (to left) goes up to the village of Pyrgos and to the Monastery of Profitis Elias (an excursion described on pp. 173-181). You stay on the main road, which starts its descent toward the southwest.

7,5 Km.: Turn-off (to right) leads down to Athinios, the small port used by most scheduled ships (p. 101).

9 Km.: The road passes alongside village of Megalokhorion, noted for several fine churches including the Ayii Anargyri and the Presentation of the Virgin Mary.

11,5 Km.: Here is the turn to the right on the asphalt road for Akrotiri.

13 Km.: This is the edge of the village of Akrotiri. It has some ruins of the Venetian fort; and outside of the town is the Church of the Archangel

Akrotiri Excavations.

Akrotiri Excavations.

Memorial where Marinotos fell to death.

(where the first Bishop of Sifnos is buried); but these will hardly deter many people from moving directly on. You bear left here at the junction and cut away from the village toward the coast (south).

14,5 Km.: The parking area of the site. A couple hundred yards further on is the sea, with decent bathing. In the summer there is a small hotel here and modest meals can be obtained at several tavernas. There is also better swimming at the red-pebbled beach along the coast; small boats take you there for a fee. Just to the right (west) of the beach, too, is the little Chapel of *Ayios Nikolaos Mavrorachidi,* tucked into the flank of an extinct volcano.

The Story of the Excavations

It seems to be one of the necessary myths of our time to envision archaeologists as wizards who descend out of nowhere, touch their magic wands to some remote plot of earth, shout "Presto!" – and a great ancient palace appears where no one expected anything. In fact the real story of more archaeological sites is far more fabulous and dramatic – or so it seems to some – and for just the opposite reasons: the remains have long cried out to be unearthed, and the archaeologist who discovers them is the one who pushes on where other have turned aside. Indeed, the discovery of a site like Akrotiri recalls the definition of most works of genius: "Inspiration – 2%. Perspiration – 98%." It is in no way to detract from the achievement of Professor Spyridon Marinatos if we tell the full background of the site; indeed, it is the story he would want told.

Perhaps the most appropriate point to begin the story of the Akrotiri excavations is, as with so much that happens on Santorini, with a volcanic eruption. This one was in January 1866 (p. 47), and as this was one of the first such phenomena to occur in the age of modern geology, it drew the attention of many scientists. Indeed, both the Greek and French governments dispatched scientists over to Santorini to study the eruption, and it was these men – not archaeologists – who first called the world's attention to the ancient remains on Santorini.

Credit for priority seems to go to a Greek professor from the University of Athens, but the background to his discovery is a fascinating footnote. The Suez Canal was then being constructed, and there was a need for large quantities of cement; since the volcanic ash of Santorini could be used to make a cement especially resistant to water, the Suez Canal Company had been working several quarries on Santorini. One such was along the southern cliffs of the island of Thirasia, and in removing the material from here the workmen had come upon some large stone blocks – man-made, obviously, and evidently the remains of walls – buried beneath the thick layer of ash. The people responsible realized in their own way that to be located here these walls must have been quite ancient, but they were more interested in obtaining the ash. And it was at this point, in 1866, that Christomanos, the Professor of chemistry, appeared from Athens; he asserted that these might be valuable archaeological remains. Two men from Santorini then started a bit of excavating at the site, actually discovering some pottery as well as the remains of a house. But the quarrying proceeded, undoubtedly destroying many valuable remains.

Meanwhile, a French scientific mission was investigating the eruption; among its members was Ferdinand Fouqué, a geologist-vulcanologist. He saw what these men had discovered on the south coast of Thirasia and during the following year (1867) he proceeded to direct a quite respectable archaeological operation: he excavated a pillar crypt and recorded the finds (including a human skeleton). Moreover, Fouqué, his interest now fired by these finds on Thirasia, began to make inquiries around Santorini, and a local farmer led him to a ravine near the village of Akrotiri on the southwest coast of the main island. Because of the erosion caused by torrents here, the deep layers of ash and pumice had been washed away, and parts of walls as well as masses of potsherds were actually visible in the slopes. Fouqué was not able to excavate in any proper sense, but he did collect enough sherds to be able to piece together some vases. He was also led to a ravine east of the first one, where he found some vaulted tombs, potsherds, obsidian blades, and gold rings.

It is interesting to note that this was taking place in 1867 – exactly one century before Professor Marinatos was to start his excavations on this very site. Of more immediate impact, Fouqué's finds inspired two French archaeologists, Mamet and Gorceix, to come over from Athens in 1870; they made a more professional study, mapping the site around the ravine and extending their excavations beyond that area. On the coast north of Akrotiri – that is, on the inner rim of the caldera – they fond house walls that had broken off at the very point where the land had collapsed into the sea; on this site they also found vases with carbonized straw, barley, lentils, and peas as well as a copper saw. Back on the ravine where Fouqué had made his finds, they found scores of vases – some painted – and in one house frescoed walls: yes, walls – and possibly ceilings – had been painted in several colors; in one section, flowers were visible. But because this particular house was still underground, they had to abandon their explorations – and the whole structure soon collapsed.

After this work in 1870, excavations on Santorini came to an end. Mamet published a fine little volume in 1874 (*De Insula Thera*), and Fouqué published a quite ambitious work in 1879 (*Santorin et ses éruptions*), to this day a standard work on the geology and vulcanology of Santorini. But the true significance of all their finds was hardly appreciated even by those most directly concerned: they had no way of knowing how old their finds were. And after all, how could they know that they had been looking at Minoan vases and Minoan-period frescoes? The Minoan civilization had yet to be discovered. (Although there, too, much more was known than is generally realized; and by coincidence, in 1878, the first excavation on the site of the palace of Knossos had even turned up some large pithoi and walls.)

But little was known of the Aegean's early history, and it was hard to fit any such random finds into a pattern. What these early workers on Santorini did, however, was to make at least a few specialists aware that Santorini had participated in some fairly ambitious culture. But this was but a very small piece of a jigsaw puzzle, the rest of whose missing parts, and their design, were still unknown. So that is where thing stood for another generation. Then, in 1896, Friedrich Hiller von Gaertringen, the German archaeologist, began to turn up the extensive remains of Ancient Thera (pp. 120-121); but as distinguished as they were, nothing dated much before 800 B.C. (and most remains were from still later centuries) and it was recognized that they had no direct connection with the Akrotiri site and its culture.

But in 1899, another German archaeologist, Zahn, influenced by Von Gaertringen's finds, came and excavated a bit at a little valley known as Potamos, just east of where the French had dug at Akrotiri. But Zahn did not produce much, nor did he publicize his work. So again, Santorini and its Akrotiri remains fell into obscurity, especially as it was in 1900 that the spotlight of archaeology shifted onto Crete, where Arthur Evans had just begun to unearth the great palace at Knossos (and the Italians had also begun to excavate the palace at Phaestos).

Almost overnight, a whole era in human culture took on definition: Evans called it the Minoan Civilization – since dated to about 2600 to 1100 B.C. – and aside from its flowering on Crete, it was soon realized that it had put out roots and tendrils elsewhere in the Mediterranean. Anyone who knew the materials discovered on Santorini would have been struck by those earlier similarities. Indeed, they would have recognized actual Minoan imports. Some scholars did note just this, but it need not have indicated much more than a small Minoan trading post on Santorini.

As the excavation of Knossos and other Minoan sites elsewhere on Crete continued, a young Greek archaeologist appeared on the scene. In 1932, Spyridon Marinatos was excavating at Amnissos (about four miles east of Iraklion), which was suspected to have served as a harbor town and arsenal for Knossos. Marinatos did find a villa there with frescoes, an important altar, and – most relevant to our story – a building with quantities of pumice in the basement. In his first published report of that year, Marinatos only hinted at some connection between this pumice and Santorini; two years later he made a more explicit connection. But it was in 1939 that Marinatos published his hypothesis for an international public in the British periodical. *Antiquity*. In an article, he set down two connecting claims: (1) The pumice at Amnissos was from a volcanic eruption of Santorini; and (2), this eruption was of such cataclysmic proportions that it overwhelmed many of the major Minoan sites on Crete and thus brought the Minoan civilization to an abrupt end. Because the hypothesis was based on relatively slight evidence, and because it conflicted with the then-prevailing theory of the Minoans' collapse – that it was due to an earthquake and/or an invasion – the editors of *Antiquity* added a note to the effect that Marinatos's theory awaited additional support from excavations at other sites.

But because of World War II and its aftermath, excavations were delayed throughout the Aegean, and during the 1950s Marinatos became involved at other sites. That pumice in the room at Amnissos continued to bother him, however, and he carried on his search in excavation reports, by examining finds from other sites, and even, as he himself puts it, by investigating "living tradition among inhabitants about old finds." Then, in the 1960s, several developments began to bring the hypothesis back into focus. Surveys by various geologists of the Mediterranean sea floor were revealing the extent of the fall-out from the great Santorini eruptions – lending support to Marinatos' claim that one cuch could have caused damage on Crete. And on Crete itself, starting in 1961, Professor Nikolaos Platon was excavating a major Minoan palace-site at Kato Zakros, in southeastern Crete – and the early published reports claimed finds of pumice there, too.

Finally, in 1962 and again in 1964, Marinatos was able to get over to Santorini to make some surveys of potential excavation areas. Two factors played the major influence in his choice of the Akrotiri ravine. Obviously, the reports and finds from the nineteenth-century excavations in the area

Big urns (Pithoi) at Akrotiri.

were crucial. But Marinatos was further drawn to this site for the same reason that had led the first searchers there: the slope of the land and the winter torrents had combined to erode much of the great layer of volcanic pumice and tephra that elsewhere attained thicknesses of over 200 feet. Here the volcanic material was at most fifty feet thick, and in places the pre-eruption level was exposed, leaving stone walls visible. Marinatos further speculated that the gentle coastal plain and the relatively shallow coastal waters at this point made it a likely locale for a settlement.

After studying all these factors, the previous maps and finds, and other evidence, Marinatos came over to Santorini in the spring of 1967 to begin the actual excavation. He sank his first trial trench on May 25, and within a few hours he and his assistants were finding fragments of painted pottery, "strongly reminiscent of Middle Cycladic pottery from other sites and even of the Kamares pottery of Crete." Then the first walls were exposed, suggesting that they had come across structures. And starting with those first fruitful hours in 1967, the excavations at Akrotiri continued to be successful beyond anyone's expectations, each summer's dig revealing more details and extensions to the settlement.

The results of this century-old search are what you will be visiting at Akrotiri (or seeing in the museum). Beyond thse tangible remains, however, are various significances and implications of the site. First, of course, is confirmation that Santorini participated in early Aegean culture – specifically in the phases known as Cycladic and Minoan. Second, it reveals specific links with the Minoan civilization of Crete, although just what this relationship was is still an open question. Then, the conditions at the site confirm the geological evidence for a cataclysmic volcanic eruption and help to fix its date; this inevitably raises questions about the effect of this same disaster on the Minoan civilization of Crete. As for any reflections all this throws on the age-old search for Atlantis, this is dealt with in some detail elsewhere (pp. 24-30).

But here we might conclude with still another implication of this site. For Professor Spyridon Marinatos, it represented the grand climax of a distinguished career: a site of dimensions granted to but few archaeologists; the vindication of a life-long devotion granted to fewer scholars; and a personal satisfaction granted to still fewer human beings on this earth. And then in 1974, an even more fateful event occurred: Marinatos was supervising some excavating when the wall he was standing on collapsed and he died of the injuries he suffered. (A memorial to Marinatos is maintained at this very spot).

But his work was taken up by another outstanding Greek archaeologist and authority in the prehistory of the Aegean, Dr. Christos Doumas, who has continued the excavations and the publishing of their results so that the Akrotiri site promises to remain one of the major centers our knowledge of Bronze Age civilization. (As of this writing, however, no inscribed tablets – Linear A, Linear B, or any kind – have been found at Akrotiri.)

History of Ancient Akrotiri

It is still far too early to attempt anything like a history of the settlement being unearthed at Akrotiri, but here we might summarize what little is known (and which is dealt with in some detail at appropriate places elsewhere in this book). A settlement began on the site perhaps as early as 3000 B.C. (p. 49), but it was not till the centuries after 2000 B.C. that it developed into an ambitious town; three-story houses, superb frescoes, public and ceremonial buildings, craft and commercial activities, and a range of material culture that had links with the Cycladic, Mycenaean, and – above all – Minoan civilizations (pp. 50-52).

Then, about 1500 B.C., an earthquake or series of earthquakes inflicted severe damage on the town (pp. 51); survivors returned and cleared away the dead and the debris, but never really rebuilt their town; instead, they took to living in the shell of its ruins in a way that has led to their being called "squatters" (p. 51). It is believed that they lived in this way, moreover, for only a short time – at most up to two or three years – when the final catastrophe overwhelmed not only this settlement but the island as a whole. The site remained buried under volcanic ash and lost to human consciousness until the excavations that began about a century ago (pp. 138-140).

Visiting the Site

The ticket booth has been located about 100 yards below the site, but subsequent excavations may have required it to relocate. However, you approach from the south, and what you first see is a rather unsightly construction: a vast shed made of metal supports (rather like a giant's erector set) and roofed with a translucent, corrugated synthetic material. All this is necessary to protect the site from the elements, wind as well as rain. (About 2 acres, or one hectare, is under cover.) Originally, Marinatos had thought he might leave much, if not all, of the remains underground: the idea was to excavate by tunneling, putting in supporting walls and roofs where necessary; visitors would then have walked through an illuminated, subterranean Pompeii. In the end, though, the layer of volcanic material did not prove thick enough to allow this (the deepest part being only about 35 feet.) So this great shed has become the compromise: it leaves the site relatively intact for archaeological studies and allows visitors to walk through a 3500-year-old town.

Since the site is still being excavated, various details will undoubtedly change, but the basic circuit will probably remain the same. (You need not always proceed around the site by this set route, but crowds will probably force you to pretty much go their way.) And a knowledge of the details is not even necessary to enjoy the site: most people are impressed, if not overwhelmed, just by stepping into the shed and seeing the extent of the remains. Thereafter, it is enough to see the familiar doorways, windows, stairways, multistoried buildings, fine ashlar (smoothed and squared) masonry, traces or wooden beams (they left only hollow "imprints," of course, which have been replaced by concrete), and the urns left *in situ* to recognize a world not that far removed from our own.

As you move in under the shed, you proceed around to the left (you are heading roughly north). Along the left side of the path is Quarter G: in the first set of rooms (note the thick walls) were found some frescoes; these rooms also provided dramatic evidence of the severe earthquake that preceded the final catastrophe. You then make a slight bend left and come onto what has been named Telchines Road: it is paved in granitic lava, polished by the footsteps of its ancient users. More rooms of Quarter G are on the left, while to the right is Room 2 of Quarter B: it is easily identified by its buckled floor, made of flagstones of lava. This was, in fact, the floor of a second-story room, which had a column in its center. The windows alongside the road belong to the lower story.

Proceeding north on Telchines Road, you pass by (on the right) the room where Marinatos fell to his death (and now treated as a memorial) and come into a fairly large open space, the North Court – enclosed by 2- and 3-storied buildings. Standing in the center of this Bronze Age plaza is surely one of the peak experiences for archaeological seekers. From here you proceed north until you come along the area known as Quarter A. At the very corner of this block is the building known as the "Mill House": it was so named because of the millstone that was found during the first digging here, but Marinatos later came to decide it might well have been a shrine (and the millstone was used to prepare flour used in sacrifices). There is a fine, preserved doorway into the anteroom of this Mill House, and a painted bathtub was found inside.

Perissa - church of Stavros.

Abandoned windmills road to Perissa.

To the east (right) of the Mill House is a large storeroom divided into three sections (on its N-S axis). It was discovered during the first year's excavations, and since it contained so many fine painted vases of various sizes (including some containing flour) it was a particularly auspicious start for the site. So many fragments of vases were found in one of the sections, in fact, that when assembled there would not have been enough space in the room to contain all the vases; it is surmised that they were being stored there in their broken condition. Also found in the storeroom were: loom weights, a bronze knife, drill, and strainer; many traces of wooden window sills and jambs; and (in a small room adjoining the middle section) the fine bull rhyton (p. 126) that has suggested this room might have been used for some religious function.

Depending on the state of the excavations when you are visiting, you will probably by this point be following a route that leads across some wooden "bridges" as you begin to circle back and head south along the eastern edge of the site. Everywhere you look there will be signs of the excavations that are still in progress – the fine ashlar masonry walls ("ashlar" referring to stones that have been carefully dressed, or cut to straight edges), the numerous large urns, the doorways. It is still something of a "work in progress" but the sheer extent and diversity of the site should impress even the most casual site-visitor. There is no need to exaggerate: it is not Pompeii. But it is an extraordinary site, and as you come back to where you entered, you will feel you have been privileged to walk through a past culture.

Perissa

The Orthodox church at Perissa – with its various historical, legendary and religious associations – is really a major shrine for the people of Santorini; summer weekend excursions to Perissa have traditionally been a combination pilgrimage and beach party. Now the beach and its attendant entrepreises – cafes, restaurants – attract so many foreigners during the peak summer season that the atmosphere has undeniably changed. There are a couple of hotels (operating between April and October) and all the usual support systems of a beach. The once restful stand of pine trees is apt to be crowded by young foreigners who turn it into their campground – and are probably unaware that they are camping right beside the church. But if you arrange your visit right – eat "off-hours," visit the church properly clothed, and stay at a far end of the beach – you can still feel that Perissa has a special atmosphere.

Chapel of Panayia above Perissa.

Inside Venetian Fort Emporion.

How to Get There

Public Buses: The buses to Perissa are several a day, in each direction – really only extensions of the buses to Emporion (below). To get the fullest advantage, it would be advisable to take an early bus to Emporion, walk the $1^1/_2$ miles to Perissa, and catch the last bus back from Perissa.

Taxis: Especially with a taxi, you can combine a visit to Perissa with the visit to Akrotiri (p. 131) and/or other sites in the southern part of the island.

Hiking: Stout walkers could go up to, or down from, the Monastery of Profitis Elias (p. 173) or Ancient Thera (p. 159).

The Trip to Perissa

Follow the route toward Akrotiri as far as the turn-off at the 11.5 Km. point (described on pp. 136). For Perissa, continue on south (that is, do *not* turn to right).

12 Km.: Set alongside the road (on left) is the little squarish chapel of Ayios Nikolaos Marmaritis (or Marmarinos) – "St. Nicholaos in Marble" – so named because it is made of marble (imported from Naxos). It can be admired from the outside and you can peek inside through the door; if you are serious about investigating its interior, you must go on another $^1/_2$ mile to Emporion and get the key from a local priest. But its history is what rewards our curiosity. It was originally a Temple to Thea Basilae ("Queen of the Gods"), erected in the 3rd century B.C.; it was of Doric style and more rectangular. (The dedicatory inscription survived on the corbel.) Eventually, Christians remodelled it and rededicated it to St. Nicholaos; they added the present doorway while using what marble remained for the square chapel. Inside they built a small alcove, or shrine, with its columns and pediment, to hold the holy image. If you look inside, you can also note the coffered marble ceiling.

12.5 Km.: A dirt road turns off to the right and leads down to Cape Exomyti, which has a good beach, a couple of restaurants, and some ancient remains scattered about the area. Some remains of harbor works are also to be seen under the sea; these are probably from the ancient port of Eleusis, which has been claimed as an ancient Phoenician settlement (p. 52) or as a port for Ancient Thera (p. 53); most likely the remains date from the later period of the Ptolemies. This part of Santorini seems to have subsided during a major earthquake in A.D. 1570.

13 Km.: Having proceded along the main road, you come to the edge of

Emporion. (If you have no interest in seeing the town, bear right and proceed along its edge.) A prosperous villager, and the second most populous on Santorini, Emporion once boasted one of the major Venetian fortresses on the island, but it has been largely destroyed by earthquakes and the elements. Some of the old houses and narrow roads, as well as the fiteenth-century Church of the Panayia, all built inside the original fortress, have survived.

13.5 Km.: Just outside of Emporion, another dirt road (on the right) leads down to Cape Exomyti (p. 152).

16 Km.: You arrive at Perissa, with its imposing Church of Stavros ("the Cross") and monastery compound. As mentioned, this is a favorite destination for both foreign campers and native pilgrims.

The background to this church involves a mixture of history and legend. Originally there was supposed to have been an old Byzantine church on this site, dedicated to Ayia Irini (patron saint of the island: p. 20). This burnt or otherwise was destroyed and its whereabouts became forgotten. Then, in the early nineteenth century, a local villager is said to have had a dream in which he was told how to go about digging up the church; the villagers found the ruins, and then proceeded to build a large, new church in the area; a monastery became attached to this to maintain the church as a shrine. Much of that church collapsed in the 1956 earthquake, and the church you see now has been erected since then. Its name (Stavros) stems from the fact that a bronze cross, along with an icon of the Virgin, was found in a well here; it is believed that water from the well cures the sick.

In ths south corner of the courtyard are substructures of a circular Roman heroon, or shrine; in the first century A.D. this was converted into a tomb for a certain Frasiclaea.

Up to the rocky cliff (which is a side of the Mesa Vouno on which Ancient Thera sits: p. 159) is the little Chapel of Panayia Zothokhopigi.

Kamari Beach

Most people now go to Kamari simply to enjoy the swimming or a few lazy hours on the beach; others come through enroute to Ancient Thera (an excursion described below in detail: p. 159-163). Kamari's beach, in fact, is probably the most frequented of Santorini's; it is a gray-black volcanic ash-and-pebble, not true sand, which at least adds to its curiosity value if not its comfort (and it can be hellishly hot to walk on during the summer days). There are now numerous cafes, tavernas and restaurants along the beach, as well as several hotels (one, the Kamari, has its private pool!) and many bungalows and rooms to rent (both along the beach and up in the village). There is a camp ground on the edge of the village, too. Waterskiing and windsurfing are also offered by vendors on the beach. As for the crowds that congregate here during the peak weeks – it's a fairly long beach, and all you have to do to avoid them is to move to one end or the other.

How to Get There

Public Buses: There are several a day, in each direction, allowing a full day at the beach.

Taxis: As the public buses can be absolutely jammed by young people during the peak weeks, here is one trip that many might prefer to make by taxi. (It is, after all, only a 10 Km. trip). You can usually count on getting a taxi back to Fira, too, especially if you leave ahead of the crowds.

Hiking: Kamari might well be treated as a way-station on walks to or from Ancient Thera (p. 159) and the Monastery of Profitis Elias (p. 173).

Fishermen at Kamari Beach.

The Trip to Kamari Beach

You set off as on the route to Akrotiri: leaving Fira by C (Town Plan: A - 10), and at 2 Km. passing the turn-off to the village of Karterados (p. 136).

3 Km.: The public bus at this point turns right off the main road and drives up a few hundred years to the edge of the village of Messaria, where it stops to leave off and pick up passnegers. Messaria prides itself on its houses and churches as well as its commercial and intellectual acumen. The bus then returns to the main road and turns off it again, this time onto a road leading east.

2 Km.: At this point you bear right for Kamari; to bear left (due east) would bring you in about another 3 Km. to the airport. Continuing on around the north edge of the airfield, you would come at 8 K, to the settlement known as Monolithos: the name refers to the 100-foot-hight solitary stone (*mono-lithos* in Greek) that is a remnat of the original pre-volcanic island that emerged when the sea rushed in (p. 40). There is a decent beach here, with bungalows to rent and food to eat. Some might prefer this to the more crowded beaches such as Kamari.

Back at the 4.5 Km. point, meanwhile, most people will have made the turn to the right continuing their trip to Kamari.

5.5 Km.: You pass below – on the slopes up to the right – the village of Vothonas.

6 Km.: A turn-off to the right leads up to the village of Mesa Gonia (and beyond that, to Exo Gonia). Gonia suffered greatly in the earthquake of 1956 (and many of its residents then abandoned it to settle in the village of Kamari) but it has made a comeback in the decades since. This road, by the way, if followed all the way up its winding, climbing course, comes out (after about 2 Km) at the edge of Pyrgos (see p. 176).

7 Km.: Another turnoff (right) leads in about a $^1/_2$ km to one of the finest and most famous churches of Santorini, the Panayia Episkopi, as it is widely known; its formal name is Church of Kimisis Theotokou (Assumption of the Virgin); but because it once served as the seat of the Orthodox Bishop of Santorini, it gained the name Episkopi (and has even lent that name to the village as a whole).

Situated against the foot of Mount Profitis Elias, the Church of the Panayia was built during the reign of the Byzantine Emperor Alexis I Comnenus in the late eleventh century; its frescoes are claimed to date from as early as 1100. When the Venetians took over the island in the thirteenth century, (p. 61), they replaced the Orthodox Bishop with a Roman Catholic Bishop. Then when the Turks took over Santorini in the sixteenth century, they returned the church to the Orthodox.

Terraced land.

View of interior.

Terraced vine-yards.

View of land.

157

Plants.

Typical vegetation.

Typical vegetation.

So-called pepper tree.

158

The church has two chapels, which are said to have been used at one stage simultaneously by the Roman Catholics and the Orthodox. The church maintains a small "museum" or collection of Byzantine icons, manuscripts, and vestments. On August 15 the feast day for the Assumption of the Virgin, hundreds of Santorinians gather here, starting on the eve before, and there is much fine eating on the day itself.

9.5 Km.: Proceeding on the main road, you come through the village of Kamari, and, taking the sharp turn to the left, proceed down to beach.

10 Km.: You arrive at the beach of Kamari. Here, by the way, it is thought by some scholars, was located ancient Oia (or Ia), a port for Ancient Thera, high above. Remains of some ancient structures have been found here, and they would seem to confirm this identification.

Ancient Thera

Here is a site that probably 999 out of 1,000 visitors to Santorini have never heard of until they arrive on the island; then, when they first hear of it, they are apt to get it confused with the more recently publicized excavations at Akrotiri (p. 138-148). All is further confused by its name – although to make that clear, we refer throughout this book to this site as Ancient Thera. Where and what is this unexpected site that people are being encouraged to visit? It is located on the peak or promontory known as Mesa Vouno, which rises to a height of 1,211 feet on the southeast corner of Santorini; the remains tend to be more at the 1,000 to 1,200 foot range and are spread along a relatively narrow "corridor" – about 450 feet wide and some 2,600 fett long – which looks south onto Perissa and north onto Kamari. Although settled from at least 800 B.C. and up to about A.D. 800, most of the remains that reward today's visitors are from the "middle phase," about 600 B.C. to A.D. 200.

But there is no use misleading people: although some of the individual remains are quite interesting it is not one of the great archaeological sites. What is spectacular is its location, high above Santorini and the sea, and what "makes" the expedition worth the effort is the total experience. Usually there are relatively few visitors on the fairly extensive site at any one time (although there is always at least one caretaker on duty) so you can stroll through the ruins and be alone with your thoughts – and the wind that usually howls about (often quite fiercely!).

When you leave the site you feel more as though you have been through some *rite de passage* than on some casual tour. And it is one of those

continue on p. 162

159

ANCIENT THERA

A To Kamari
B To Profitis Elias Monastery
C To Perissa

1. Agios Stephanos (Basilica of Archangel Michael)
2. Tombs
3. Byzantine Gate
4. Byzantine Fortifications
5. Archaic Necropolis
6. Votive Niche of Demeter and Kore (Pitaros Cave)
7. Christos Cave-Chapel
8. Temenos of Artemidorus
9. Governor's (Commandant's) Palace
10. Garrison Gymnasium
11. Temple of Dionysus
12. Platys Teikhos
13. Agoras (North & South)
14. Royal Portico (Stoa Basilika)
15. Incised phallus
16. Residence of Ptolemy the Benefactor (Basilistai House)
17. Sanctuary of Egyptian Gods (Isis, Anubis, Serapis)
18. Byzantine Church (Temple of Pythian Apollo)
19. Theater
20. Sacred Way
21. Baths
22. Church of Annunciation
23. Heroon and Rotunda
24. Sanctuary (Tomb) of Ptolemy III
25. Temple of Apollo Karneios
26. Heroon of Theras
27. Terrace of Festivals
28. Baths
29. Gymnasium of Epheboi (Youths)
30. Grotto of Hermes and Herakles
31. Dedicatory Inscriptions

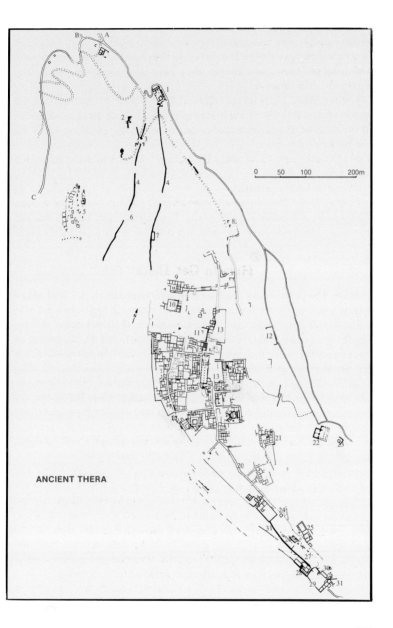

ANCIENT THERA

archaeological sites, too, that inevitably raise thoughs about the extremes to which men have driven themselves in their search for security, power, and prestige. How these people must have felt "monarchs of all they surveyed." Yet today -?

Visiting Hours: Daily (excpt holidays) 8:30 - 3:00. But note that no one is admitted after 2:30 since there is a fairly long walk along the ridge just to get to the remains. The caretakers are strict about moving everyone out of the site by 3.

No Entrance Fee: (You might tip the caretaker if you make use of his services).

Photographs: Unrestricted.

Visiting Time: Most peole will want about 1-$1^1/_2$ hours to poke around the remains; depending on your means of getting there (see below), you will be able to calculate how much time you need for the complete excursion.

How to Get There

Buses: The public buses run only to Kamari (see above, p. 154); once at Kamari, you might find a taxi there to take you up to the site but you cannot count on it. There are tour buses, however, that operate out of Fira, and for many people this is probably the recommended way of getting to this remote site. Even so, it must be said, there is a fairly arduous walk from the parking lot to the remains.

Taxis: As stated above, you might find a taxi in Kamari, but most people who want to go this way will have hired the taxi in Fira. Make sure the driver is willing to go all the way up to site (as the road is bumpy: see below) and also wait for you.

Mopeds, Motorbikes: As long as the vehicle has enough power (and you are not too heavy) these can make it up to the parking lot.

Hiking: Most people who decide to walk up to Ancient Thera will probably be coming from Kamari; it's only about a 2 Km. walk from the village, but it's a relatively steep (and at places rough) walk. Those in good condition will probably need no more than a half hour to get up, while others will want to take a more leisurely pace. (Bring your own water!) Another approach is to come down over the Sellada Pass from the Monastery of Profitis Elias (p. 173) – a walk of an hour's duration and not for everyone. Still another approach is to come up from Perissa (p. 152) - a quite ambitious uphill climb of at least an hour's duration. After visiting the site of Ancient Thera, you can walk on to any of these destinations, but most people will probably head down for Kamari – an easy half hour after your exertions in getting up to Ancient Thera.

Approaching Ancient Thera

The first part of the trip – assuming, that is, you are setting out from Fira – is the trip to Kamari Beach described on pp. 153-159.

Once at Kamari, you will then be either taxiing or walking up, but before setting off you might like to take a moment to look up and get oriented. With your back to the sea, you face the mountainous promontory of Mesa Vouno, rising steeply out of the sea to the left; if you follow the high ridge rightwards to the point where it comes to an abrupt end and drops to a "saddle" – that is where you are heading: the entrance to the site is at about that point, and the remains (some of which can in fact be seen from Kamari) stretch along the high ridge. A banked and terraced road curves up to the point where the "saddle" meets the ridge; the road has been paved in rough stone partway up; it comes to an end at a small parking circle. The gate and fence indicating the site are visible from this point, up to the left, and from here everyone must proceed on foot.

History of Ancient Thera

Ancient Thera's earliest history may have begun with the first settlers on Santorini (pp. 49), yet nothing has ever been found to link this site with the Cycladic period sites around Santorini, such as at Akrotiri. Early people certainly sought out high places for safety and health, but this peak was probably too much of a good thing. The first people known to have come up here were the Dorian colonists, who founded one of their seven settlements on Santorini here, naming it after their leader, Theras (pp. 53). This might have been as early as 900 B.C., although nothing from that early has been identified; the earliest tombs in the area date from closer to 800 B.C.

Certainly by about 700 B.C., Ancient Thera seems to have been flourishing, as evidenced by the many tombs and various graffiti (inscriptions in the rock) that date from the following century. These inscriptions, by the way, are among the earliest Archaic Greek inscriptions known, and they reflect a Dorian culture like Sparta's (p. 54). By the last third of the seventh century the Ancient Therans must have been so enterprising that they sent a colonial expedition off to North Africa where they founded Cyrene (in modern Libya). This was in 631-630 B.C., and then in 571 B.C. more Therans went off to replenish the colony (and Cyrene grew to become, in many respects, a more ambitious community than its motherland). It is assumed that the years between about 630-570 B.C. represent the "flowering" of Ancient Thera, and several of the major public structures are dated to this period: the Heroon of Theras (p. 172), the Temple of Apollo Karneios (p. 172), and the Terrace of Festivals (p. 55).

The history of Ancient Thera during the Classical Age of Greece has been told as part of the large history of Santorini (p. 152): what it comes to is that Santorini's ties to Dorian Sparta seem to have influenced it to resist – or at least to refuse to cooperate with – the Attic-Athenian exertions. By about 430 B.C., Santorini was nevertheless essentially subservient to Athens, but there are no remains or indications that Ancient Thera contributed to "the golden age" of ancient Greece.

Ancient Thera's next moment in the sun, rather, came in the Hellenistic era after 300 B.C. Alexander the Great had died (323 B.C.) and his empire had been divided up by his generals; Ptolemy, a Macedonian Greek, had taken over Egypt and initiated a dynasty of Graeco - Egyptian rulers. These Ptolemies were anxious to maintain their own "mini-empire", and desirous of keeping watch over their interests in the Aegean, they established a naval station on Santorini. For the actual port, they seem to have selected a site on the modern beach of Kamari, which they called Oia; at some point, too, they may also have set up a port at Eleusis, at Cape Exomyti, the other side of Mesa Vouno (p. 55). But as the "capital" of the island and headquarters of their naval interests, they chose the already existent Greek community of Ancient Thera, on the top of Mesa Vouno. They dispatched a garrison here and sent on a series of commanders, and during the reign of the first three Ptolemies (pp. 55), Ancient Thera became a quite ambitious place; many of the remains we see today date from that century. But although this was, on the one hand, a rather exotic, cosmopolitan community (the Ptolemies, for instance, introduced the worship of Egyptian deities: p. 55), a strong Greek bedrock was there. Indeed, that is exactly what Hellenistic culture was: a mixture of Greek with foreign elements.

The Macedonian Antigonids displaced the Ptolemies in the Aegean for a brief spell (p. 172), but when the Romans took over the Greek world from the end of the third century B.C. on, they cleared out the Macedonians and took over at least nominal control of Ancient Thera. They built some structures (such as the baths: p. 172), but they seem to have contented themselves mainly with restoring and adapting the Hellenistic structures (such as the theater: p. 169, or the Royal Portico: p. 169). The fact is that a place like Ancient Thera did not figure very prominently in Rome's imperial visions.

Then it was Rome's turn to decline, and in A.D. 395, its grand empire was divided into two; Santorini naturally became part of the eastern, Byzantine Empire. And it was about this same time, too, that another influence appeared on Santorini: Christianity. (According to an inscription at Ancient Thera, in fact, it came at the end of the fourth century: p. 168). The Christians built some churches at Ancient Thera, but often they simply converted pagan temples and sacred places into their own (as with the Temple of Pythian Apollo: p. 172, or the Christos Cave: p. 169). What new structures the Byzantines built were principally fortifications - indicative of the fearful state of life in those "dark ages." Ancient Thera seems never to have attracted any major assault but simply faded away, and when the Venetians came in the thirteenth century, they paid the site its final insult - and simply ignored it.

Excavating Ancient Thera

There had been various finds and excavations on Santorini since 1866 (pp. 138), enough to establish that the island had been inhabited in ancient times. And although not much was known about the age or duration of these finds, they were recognized as being extremely old, both by virtue of their location underneath the volcanic ash and by the absence of any signs of written script. So it was that when reports of inscriptions on some exposed rocks on top of Mesa Vouno came to the attention of the German Baron, Friedrich Hiller von Gaertringen, at the end of the nineteenth century, he realized that this site was not contemporaneous with the remains earlier explored by the Greek and French. And what brought him to Santorini in 1896 were these very inscriptions . (Similarly, Arthur Evans about this very time was first attracted to Crete by his interest in some script he had found on Cretan sealstones.) Still a young man (1864 - 1947 were his dates: incidentally, he lived to see his nephew Konrad Adenauer emerge as a leader of post-war Germany), independently wealthy (like so many of the early diggers), Von Gaertringen was working on a German collection of all known Greek inscriptions.

At first he concentrated on the inscriptions on the exposed rocks. They were recorded in an Archaic Greek, and as such were among the oldest examples of the Greek alphabet. They were also written in the so-called **boustrophedon** or "ox-plow", script: that is, lines alternated from left - to - right and right -to - left, with the words of the latter written in reverse order, with their letters in a kind of mirror - writing. (Another well - known example of this ox - plow script is the Law Code of Gortyna, on Crete; it is dated to about 500 B.C.). The inscriptions could be dated to about the seventh century (700 - 600 B.C.) and they could be read; many seemed to be of an erotic nature and indicated homosexual sentiments. Von Gaertringen transcribed them by painting the rough, eroded letters with water color; he then pressed oiled paper over and took their imprints.

Von Gaertringen was achieving his initial aim, then, but he also realized he could not fully place these inscriptions until he knew something more about the people who put them there. So he decided to dig a bit in the area, and within the first hour and half he was uncovering more rock-cut inscriptions and traces of structures. As he proceeded to dig farther and farther from the original area, he began to uncover more and more remains. Over the years – he continued to dig until 1903 – Von Gaertringen uncovered the remains of many centuries and several cultures, spread along the ridge for about 2,600 feet and to a width of about 450 feet. Some of the remains, moreover, were under layers of pumice and ash many feet thick (from the eruptions of the last 1,000 years, of course).

It was not easy excavating such a remote site in those days; everything needed had to be taken up on mules, and all the finds were taken down on sledges and then over the dirt roads to Fira. The wind could get so strong that work often had to shift from one side of the ridge to another to avoid it. (The wind even blew one mule, loaded with ancient pottery, off the mountain to its death.) The local men who did the work erected stone huts for themselves to live in during the digging; Von Gaertringen and his assistant tried tents at first, but had to spend much time living in a deserted chapel. But Von Gaertringen enjoyed good relations with his workmen; they made him an honorary citizen; and after the theater was uncovered (p. 172), the uniformed band from Fira went all the way up there to give a concert.

In addition to the many architectural remains and the inscriptions Von Gaertringen found a lot of coins and much pottery (this in the extensive series of tombs, some going back to about 800 B.C.). He published his finds (at his own expense) in a four-volume work, *Thera* (Berlin, 1889 - 1904). Most all the removable finds are in the Fira Museum (pp. 127) or in the National Archaeological Museum in Athens.

View at airfield from road to Ancient Thera.

The road to Ancient Thera.

167

Visiting the Site

There are so many remains scattered about this site – tombs, Byzantine walls, Roman baths, etc. – that it would take a book in itself to describe them all. On the Sellada Pass, for instance, the slopping hill that joins the Mesa Vouno to the peak of Profitis Elias to the northwest, excavations that began in the early 1960s have revealed an extensive network of cemeteries from the Geometric through Roman periods, with countless funerary objects – including many fine vases, small bronzes, etc. As it happens, the most extraordinary object was discovered in 1982, the final season of the excavation program: a large pottery model of a building, very likely a shrine, made with considerable details and painted ornaments; there were also some 100 miniature vases with it. (The model stands some 15 inches high and 24 inches long, and can be seen along with the other more notable finds from the Sellada excavations in the Museum of Historic Cultures in Fira: p. 127).

The remains on the site, however, offer nothing to the average visitor, so we shall proceed on to Ancient Thera.

You come up the rather steep path to the entrance gate and pass through, climbing still higher up to winding path; as you look to your right, a bit down the slope, you will note the caretaker's house. But you take aim on the small, rather crude chapel at the top of the trail: this is the *Chapel of Ayios Stefanos* (1) (all numbers in this description of Ancient Thera refer to the site plan on p. 160-161). It was built over the ruins of a fourth-fifth century (A.D.) Basilica dedicated to the Archangel St. Michael; an inscription found here claims that Christianity came to Santorini only in the fourth century.

You now move on, generally staying along the northeast flank (consult the site plan, p. 161, to see the relationships) until after about 200 yards you come to a rocky outcrop that has been leveled off, with a low rock-face rising perpendicularly along the right. This is the *Temenos of Artemidorus of Pergae* (8) Temenos is simply a sacred enclosure or area; Artemidorus is the third century B.C. man responsible for this place; Pergae is the town in Asia Minor where he was born. He fought for Ptolemy II Philadelphus in the Arabian Desert campaigns, and then served as an admiral for the Ptolemaic fleet stationed at Santorini; something about this site must have engaged him, since he stayed on after his retirement, commissioned this elaborate shrine, and died here. Artemidorus is a typical Hellenistic figure in his cosmopolitanism, his eclecticism, his pretensions to culture and religion. One legend was that Apollo came to him as he slept and told him to erect a temple to be dedicated to various deities. Whatever his inspiration, Artemidorus had carved in the rock-face here a whole series of reliefs; some are more easily seen than others, all varying somewhat with the angle of the sun and viewer. There is the eagle of Zeus, the lion of Apollo, the altar of Concord (*Omonia*), and symbols of the Dioskouri, Hecate, and Priapus (with inscriptions and carvings that emphasize his sexual powers). And above the dolphin of Poseidon is a medallion depicting Artemidorus himself, crowned in laurel; around this is an inscription reading: "The city of the Therans has crowned Artemidorus the Theran and proclaims him a faultless citizen."

Well, it is certainly one of the more unexpected encounters on this island, and after you have contemplated it all, you proceed on until you come to a narrow, stepped road on the right (west); this you take, up to the structure erected by the Ptolemaic garrison: the *Governor's* (or *Commandant's*) *Palace* (9), on the high point of the whole site; and the *Gymnasium* (10) (in small rooms of which were found traces of red paint on the walls). Behind and lower down (to the north, that is) is a small grotto or cave that had been carved out of the rock; later the Christians converted it into the *Chapel of Christos* (7). Still father north, and on higher ground, is the *Votive Niche of Demeter and Kore* (6); this is at the entrance to a large cave, called Pitaros, and there is a throne carved out of the rock here. The association of Demeter and Kore with a cave has to do, of course, with the myth of Persephone's goings and comings from the realm of Hades.

Going down onto the lower, southern flank, you enter the north section of the *Agora* (13); once lined with shops, its two parts extend for 120 yards and vary in width from 18 to 33 yards. On the terrace to the right was the *Temple of Dionysus* (11); while if you look down onto the lower slope you will see the remains of a bastion, the *Platys Teikhos* ("broad wall") (12); its function at this point has never been fully accounted for.

As you move into the southern section of the Agora, you come alongside, on the right, the *Royal Portico* (or *Stoa Basilika*) (14). This was apparently erected by one of the Ptolemeis in the third century B.C.; it was restored by the Romans during the reign of Trajan (A.D. 98-117) and more alterations were made about A.D. 150. (This is known from the marble plaques found inside thanking the Roman benefactors.) Some 132 feet by 33 feet, it has an interior colonnade of Doric free-standing column and rows of columns set against the walls.

Up above the Royal Portico are blocks of houses from the Hellenistic period; some of these had cisterns and toilets and were decorated with mosaics. On the corner stone of one (15) is engraved a phallus with the

Royal Portico (or Stoa Basilika).

Amfitheather of Ancient Thera.

Ancient Thera.

inscription: "To my friends." (Oh well, what would *you* do for fun if you lived up here?)

Proceeding along the road out of the Agora, you come alongside, to the left, the *Theater* (19). This was erected under the Ptolemies, but the Romans adapted it, adding among other elements a proscenium. Imagine seeing a performance of a play here, looking down onto the sea, some 1,000 feet below.

Under the stage area, by the way, is a cistern, to collect rainwater as it drains from the amphitheater. There are scores of cisterns at Ancient Thera – as necessary then as they are today (p. 36). The ancient cisterns were rectangular so that they could more easily be covered with flat stones; some of them were so large that they had to have interior supporting columns. Aside from saving life-giving water, these cisterns also kept it relatively cool during the summer.

Opposite the Theater, a path leads up the slope to the *Residence of Ptolemy the Benefactor* (or *Basilistai House*) (16). Still beyond this are the remains of a Byzantine church that was built over the *Temple of Pythian Apollo* (18). Still father (a bit to the northwest) was the *Sanctuary of the Egyptian Gods* (17), with the small niches carved out of the rock. Dedicated to Isis, Anubis, and Serapis, such a temple is not at all unusual in the Hellenistic world, open as it was to so many cultural influences; remember, too, that the Ptolemies, although of Greek descent, were based in Egypt.

Descending back down to the slope that leads southeast toward the outer promontory, you proceed along the *Sacred Way* (20). Below and to the east are remains of some *Roman Baths* (21); and still farther below is the little Byzantine *Church of the Annunciation* (22) and the remains of a *Heroon* (or shrine) built over an Archaic Rotunda (23). Proceeding on, you pass (on the right) the ruins of a small *Sanctuary (Tomb) of Ptolemy III* (24) and arrive alongside the remains of the *Temple of Apollo Karneios* ("the ram") (25), so named because it was dedicated to Apollo as guardian of the flocks. Believed to date from sometime between 630-570 B.C. – the heyday of the Dorian community – the temple was some 105 feet by 33 feet. A gate on the southwest led into an inner court (with a cistern); to the southeast was a single room; to the northwest, the pronaos and cella; while on the northwest side were two little rooms (their walls and doorways still relatively intact).

Up above the temple, slightly to the west, is an oblong structure of an undetermined date; it been designated as the *Heroon* (or shrine) *of Theras* (26), after the eponymous founder of the Dorian colony on Santorini (p. 53).

You move on now to the *Terrace of the Festivals* (27), with its view down across some *Roman Baths* (28), with Perissa (p. 148) far below and the Cape Akrotiri extending off to the west. This terrace dates from the sixth century B.C.; it is supported by a retaining wall of fine stonework (which would have to be viewed from below). Here on this terrace is where the Dorians celebrated the Gymnopaedia, or "dances of youths": nude young men danced at the festivals to honor Apollo Karneios. Their admirers would carve the names of the dancers and gods – accompanied by mildly erotic epigrams – into the surroundig rock, and some of these inscriptions are to be seen in this area (31). (If you are finding it hard to fit such a practice into your experience: think of the graffiti that would get written on walls, posters, etc. after a concert by some modern Rock musicians.)

Just below the terrace, to the east, is the *Grotto of Hermes and Herakles* (30), a natural cave but with its entrance framed by hewn stone. Inside the cave is a hole from which warm air issues even during the cold winter. Hermes and Herakles were the patron deities of the young men who disported themselves here. And at the farthest extremity of the site is the *Gymnasium of the Epheboi* (or Youths) (29). Its large courtyard has various inscriptions as well as the carved outlines of feet; around the courtyard are locted a staircase, a rotunda, and various rooms.

Having completed the tour of Ancient Thera, you may now make your way back through to the point of entry and proceed on to any of several destinations.

Profitis Elias:

The Mountain and Monastery

This has long been one of the favorite goals of both the natives and visitors on Santorini. Situated on the highest peak of the island – at 1,863 feet – it enjoys a quite dramatic view over Santorini and the neighboring Aegean islands; on clear days, you are said to be able to make out the peaks of Crete, some 68 miles to the south. The monastery and its church are not especially old or architecturally distinguished, nor are its icons or other works particularly notable. But what is here is well displayed to inform the visitor – there is even a little "museum" of ecclesiastical and historical objects – and the monks make everyone feel welcome.

Visiting Hours: You can probably visit the monastery and church almost any hour, seven days a week (although remember that all Greeks respect the afternoon siesta). The little museum, however, has its hours posted:

Interior views of the Profitis Elias Monastery.

Profitis Elias Monastery.

Daily: 8 - 1, 2:30 - sunset.

It is an especially dramatic place to be at sunset, if you could so time your visit.

Festival: On July 20, people from all over Santorini come up to join the monks in celebrating the name day of Profitis Elias with dancing, feasting, and wine-drinking. Foreigners are welcomed.

How to Get There

Buses: The public buses go only as far as Pyrgos; from the village center it is another solid 3 Km. of walking – uphill all the way, but the road is good. Tour buses, of course, will take you all the way.

Taxis: You can count on getting a taxi in Pyrgos, of course, and combining this with other forms or transportation – bus or hiking. With a taxi from Fira, Profitis Elias can be combined with a larger excursion (p. 76).

Hiking: As well as walking from or to Pyrgos, you could hike to or from Perissa or Ancient Thera.

The Trip to Profitis Elias

You leave Fira by C and follow the same route as described for Akrotiri (pp. 136) as far as:

7 Km.: The turn off (to left) goes up toward the village of Pyrgos.

7.5 Km.: Just before the village "gate," a turn-off (to left) is a road that leads down to Kamari by way of the villages of Gonia (p. 155) and the Church known as Episkopi (p. 155). At the gate, you bear right and proceed around the edge of *Pyrgos*. The village has some fine old houses, the remains of a Venetian castle on the hilltop, and several Byzantine churches; the most notable is the *Theatokaki*, with some frescoes. On the rocky cliffs below the village are the little *Church of Ayios Georgios* and the *Katefio Cave*.

8.5 Km.: As you leave the far edge of the village, another footpath (to the left) leads along the slopes to the Monastery of Profitis Elias and over to Ancient Thera (p. 159) via the Sellada Pass.

You continue on the main, asphalt road, which curves and climbs up through increasingly barren terrain – although tomato plants are cultivated on the terraced land along the slopes.

12 Km.: You arrive at the monastery – now sharing the mountain top with a NATO radar station (and you are free to speculate whether it is p.

The marvelous bell-tower of Profitis Elias Monastery.

View to north (Messaria in foreground) from Profitis Elias.

Burnt Isles in center Thirasia in background.

NATO's or the monks' "vibes" that will save us yet). Passing through the monastery's unusual tower-doorway, with its tiers of bells, you come up onto the terrace from which you may enjoy the view.

Not so incidentally, it may or may not have struck you that many of the chapels and monasteries on mountan peaks throughout Greece are named after Profitis Elias or Ayios Elias. Those who know their Bible will hardly need an explanation, but some of us might like to be reminded that it's to be found in *I Kings*. Elias is, of course, Elijah, one of the major prophets of ancient Israel, and he was involved in several episodes associated with mountains. Once (Chap. 18) he stood on Mt. Carmel and called on his God to set fire to a bull he had doused in water; God did this, thus proving His superiority to the diety of the idolaters. (Mark Twain suggested that Elijah had poured oil, and when no one was looking, put a match to it). But it was another incident (Chap. 19) that inspires these many chapels and monasteries. Elijah had gone up "unto Horeb, the mount of God," and there, after a great storm, earthquake, and fire, God spoke to Elijah in "a still, small voice."

About visiting the monastery, its church, and museum: women who have too much flesh showing on their upper body will be given a shawl to wrap around it. And although there is no fee for the church or museum, it is traditional to drop a few Drachmas into one of the offertory boxes. Another way to express your appreciation is to purchase some little item in the gift shop attached to the museum (p. 181).

The original church was erected here between 1711-24, after two brothers from Pyrgos, Gabriel and Joachim, both monks, collected some money and built a small church on the peak. In 1851 King Otho of Greece visited the church and was so impressed that he suggested a monastery be added. The church is essentially one nave, with a small chapel off to the right; each with its fine old wooden iconostasis (partition). The monks provide you with a little description of their church's history and its "treasures" – in English, French, and German versions – and the icons are identified. As mentioned, nothing is that old or aesthetic, but it is nice to be informed.

After you leave the church, you may visit the museum: it is well worth the 15-20 minutes it takes to stroll through it. The monk in attendance will direct you across the courtyard and up the stairs – where you will hardly be able to miss the model of the monastery.

The Museum

First Room: Here are eccesiastical vestments; chalices and lamps; bishops' staffs; relics of saints; an iron cross used by the Crusaders; and when on display, a diamond-incrusted miter and scepter of the Ecumenical Patriarch Gregory V.

Second Room: Off the side of the first is a small room with old glassware, porcelain, and other household objects. Here, too, is the small shop maintained by the monks, with reproductions of icons, postcards, belts, and several other items for sale.

Third Room: From this small room, you descend downstairs and come into a room with a display of domestic and farm utensils that give some idea of how monks and villagers of years past lived.

Fourth Room: Beside that room is another large one with: old desks and other furnishings; church and civil documents; engravings; a seventeenth-century carved wooden ciborium; etc.

You step out into the courtyard, with various inscribed and carved stones lying about.

Kaimeni (Burnt) Isles and Thirasia

This excursion has been offered for some years now – during the tourist season only (April to October). You can hire a boat on your own at any time throughout the year, but it is certainly cheaper and more festive to go with a group. The specific goals are a first-hand glimpse at the dormant volcanic islet of Nea Kaimeni, and the chance to see something of Thirasia, the second largest island of the Santorini group. But as with all such outings, it's the total experience that makes it enjoyable. And if you've gone to the touble of getting to Santorini, you certainly might as well go all the way to volcano's mouth.

Schedule and Fees: There are numerous excursions offered with varying times and fees and everyone should find one suitable to the time and money available. At least take the simplest ride out to Nea Kaimeni, or Great Kaimeni, to see the volcanic island in progress. If you have a bit more time, take the one that includes a dip in the volcanically warmed water off Palea Kaimeni (although you must be a good swimmer, as the ship only goes within about 200 meters of the "pool"). If you have plenty of time, take the fuller excursions – those that go on to Thirasia and/or Oia or other points around Santorini. The many tourist agencies and shiplines around Fira (or your hotel) will be glad to sell you a ticket.

Special Preparations: Assuming it is a normally sunny summer's day, you will want some kind of headgear and proper shoes: you will be walking over the volcanic ash and rocks, and although that is not hot it can be heavy going on sandals or novelty shoes. Sunglasses and cameras are optional. Bring your swim-suit and towel if you expect to go swimming. And if you expect to get hungry, bring something of your own; you may stop for a cold drink, but little else.

The boat tries to depart promptly at the announced hour, so you should allow yourself the time to walk down to Fira's port. (It will probably be at a time of morning when you could always make arrangements with one the night before). Whenever you arise from your bed, remember that it takes about 15-20 minutes for the average person to walk down the long flight of stairs.

The Excursion

The boat heads first for Nea Kaimeni (sometimes known as "Great Kaimeni"); it is a 15-20 minute ride before the boat puts you ashore on the little dock in Petroulion Bay. Usually an hour's stop is scheduled, giving

Little Kamari.

average walkers just time to walk up to view the peak of the islet, King George I Crater (about 430 feet). It's about a 30 - minute walk and it can be hot under the sun; don't be ashamed to quit enroute if you find it a strain: you can examine none of the smaller cones and look for multi-colored volcanic stones. Here and there you see small patches of vegetagion that have taken hold, but mostly it is nothing but a landscape of volcanic ash and lava, broken by various craters, ravines, fissures, and fumaroles; you gain some impression of how Nea Kaimeni has grown since it first appeared in A.D. 1707. At the top, you look down into the King George I crater with sulfurous fumes and vapors coming out of fissures in its crust; you should be able to find some intersting sulfur crystals; you should be able to find some interesting sulfur crystals and colored rocks around the rim. There is not time for an extended exploration, though, and you must allow about 15-20 minutes to get back to the boat. All in all, it's quite an experience, especially if you haven't had the chance to visit one of the more spectacular volcanoes. People start off in a jaunty holiday mood and gradually become subdued by the total silence and devastation: dark and lifeless, it's the closest most of us will get to the moon.

Where you go next depends on which excursion you have signed up for. Some will head back to Fira. Others may go on around to Palea Kaimeni where the ship stops about 200 meters offshore from a small inlet where the water is warmed – and made muddy, murky, and somewhat distasteful! – by underwater volcanic springs: it is traditional to swim over and frolic in the water for a few minutes before heading back to the ship and then sailing back to Fira.

Some people will have signed on for the longer excursion to Thirasia, another 20-minute ride to the islet to the west of the main island; the ship put in at the little port settlement of Manolas. Thirasia is some three miles long and about $1^1/_2$ miles wide; along its southern coast were the volcanic ash quarries where the first signs of ancient settlers were discovered (p. 47); and some remains of an Archaic settlement (Therasia) have been found on the northern end of the island; but there is really nothing here for the casual visitor. Depending on how long the excursion boat stops here – probably about $1^1/_2$ hours – you may want to walk up to see the village of Potamos; it's a 15-20 minute walk, and when you arrive it's nothing that spectacular; but it's picturesque and is about as untouched by modern civilization as any place you'll be for a while. Some people prefer, though, to stay on the beach and swim.

Again, most excursions now head straight back to Fira, but some might go on to the port of Oia, the northernmost town on the main island of

Fishing-boats at the port of Oia.

Ancient Thira, Rock Carving.

A view of Oia.

Fira as seen from Oia.

Santorini (below). It is about a 30-minute boat ride from Thirasia, and as you approach the little port – Armeni is its official name – you see the tiny islet separated by a narrow channel from the main island: on it is the little chapel of Ayios Nikolaos.

The town of Oia is best left for a visit from overland (an excursion described below); the walk up there and back would take the better part of an hour. Most people are content to sit and have a cold drink at the café and watch the local fishermen and boat-builders.

The return trip to Fira's port is a solid 40 minutes, but it give a chance to get a good view of Santorini. And as the ship pulls in closer, it provides one of the best "photo opportunities" for many visitors to the island.

Oia

As recently as the mid-1970s, this guidebook could state that an excursion to Oia is one that "most visitors to Santorini don't get around to making." Now Oia is the mecca of countless foreigners – drawn there probably because it seems to offer an alternative to the "touristified" Fira. There is a youth hostel at Oia, and there are the much publicized "traditional village" houses (see below for details) but except for a few cafes and tavernas, Oia is certainly far less "developed" than Fira and the popular beaches. There's neither a beach nor an archaeological site near Oia, so it's a place that attracts those who like to pass their vacation in a town atmosphere – a small town, at that. And the fact is that Fira is not that far away.

How to Get There

Buses: There are a few daily public buses between Oia and Fira. And now there are tour buses that bring groups to Oia.

Taxis: Here is one of those times you should splurge on a taxi; it is really the only way you can stop to see points of interest along the way; and with a cooperative driver and a bit of Greek, you will get a guided tour for your money.

Hiking: There is an old footpath that goes along the (western) coastal cliffs; it joins the new road at Finikia (about the 10.9 Km. point); it would be about a $2^1/_2$ hour walk, one way. (And you could count on finding a taxi in Oia that would be returning to Fira.)

Traditional detail of a Santorinian house.

Visiting Oia

Although it is possible to take the lower road out of the east side of Fira and join the upper road outside of Merovigli (see at 2.2. Km., below), most people will prefer to leave Fira by the 25th of March Street (see A, Town Plan, A-5).

1 Km.: In the area of Fira known as Firostefani, of to the left, is the Monastery and Church of Ayios Gerasimos.

1.6 Km.: On the left is the Convent of Ayios Nikolaos, built in 1674; it boasts of fine old icons. Behind its fortlike walls, it sits high (1,175 feet) along the rime of the caldera. There are about a half-dozen Orthodox nuns still residing here.

2.2 Km.: Turn off the main road here, left, for a stop in the village of Merovigli (meaning "day-guard"). In the town square is the Church of the Panayia Maltese – so named because its icon of the Virgin was found in the sea off Malta; like virtually all the buildings along this route, the church had to be rebuilt after the 1956 earthquake.

But the real purpose for stopping at Merovigli is to step over to the very western edge of the village – to the very rim of the caldera, so to speak – and gaze down onto the steep (about 1,000 foot) rocky promontory known as Skaros, crowned with a few ruins of its Venetian glory. Although it is possible to climb the peak, it is far too ambitious an undertaking for most people, who will be content to stand and contemplate its history from afar. There seems to be some question as to the origin of the name of this place; one legend is that a member of the ancient Roman family of the Scauri was exiled on Santorini and settled here. What is certain is that in the early thirteenth century, after the Venetians took over Santorini, they selected this promontory as the site for one of their more powerful forts (*La Rocca*). Located on the peak, the fort was virtually impregnable and commanded a strategic view over the bay and its approaches. Skaros soon came to serve as the capital of the island, in fact, and on a somewhat lower level there grew up another castle as a residence for the aristocrats and a Roman Catholic bishop. After the Turkish came in the sixteenth century, Skaros lost its importance, although at the very end of the century a Catholic convent was established there. The story is that a maid had a dream in which St. Catherine gave a sign that a convent was to be founded there; it became quite famous in its day, attracting nuns from as far away as France; by the first quarter of the nineteenth century, though, the nuns had to abandon Skaros and they moved into a new convent, now part of the Roman Catholic compound in Fira (p. 114). By the nineteenth century, all

Passengers getting off below Oia.

the Venetian structures on Skaros were going to ruin, and today they are little more than broken walls, all but melded with the natural rock.

2.2 Km.: This is back at the point where we turned off for Merovigli and Skaros; now we proceed on, driving along the curving road that looks down onto the eastern slopes and the sea.

5.6 Km.: At about this point you should have a good view of Megalo Vouno, the highest peak (at 1,902 feet) in the northern part of Santorini.

8.6 Km.: About here you should be able to look over to the east (right) and on the outermost slope of a rocky ridge you see the little white Chapel of Panayia. On the coast nearby is the little port of Pori; and in this are two quite impressive caves (but they have to be sought out with a local guide), both of which have some obviously old, man-made constructions within.

9 Km.: There is a path that leads down (to right), about here to the Cape Kouloumbos; rock-hewn Archaic tombs were found here, and a few other fragmentary remains can be seen. It was just off this coast that the great earthquake, explosion, and subsidence of A.D. 1650 occured.

10.9 Km.: You pass along the edge of the village of Finikia (also known as Ayios Georgios).

11.6 Km.: You arrive at Oia (also transliterated as Oya, Ia, Oea). This village's name was for long Apano Meria, but in a somewhat confusing gesture it was officialy renamed Oia in honor of the port of Ancient Thera – now thought to be on the site of present-day Kamari Beach (p. 159). Oia was long one of the largest towns on Santorini, the home of many famed Greek mariners and ship-owners, but it was so seriously damaged in the 1956 earthquake that for many years thereafter it seemed to be close to abandoned. Its population declined to a few hundred, houses and other structures lay in ruin and vegetation began to take over: there was a desolate air to Oia well into the mid-1970s, a sense of being at the end of the line.

But then tourists discovered Santorini and soon their numbers began to "spill over" from the more obvious attractions. Oia and a few other locales became retreats from these more popular places. The big boost came, however, in the early 1980s, when the Greek National Tourist Organization began to restore and renovate some of the abandoned houses in Oia; decorated in a traditional Cycladic-style, furnished with all the basics (including stove, refrigerator, heater, tableware, linens, etc.), these village houses can be rented by anyone (but are now booked well in advance during the high season). If you are interested, contact the National Tourist Organziation (or if you are in a hurry, call the office in Oia: 0286-71234).

For groups of 2 to 4 people, this is both an ideal and economical way to enjoy Santorini. There are several other hotels, pensions, and rooms to rent – as well as a youth hostel – in Oia, and it can be used as a base to walk around and explore the little known parts of northernmost Santorini.

Oia itself does not claim any major cultural attractions but it has a few that would reward a visit. There is a ruined old Italian fortress that sits on a promontory at the edge of town. There is a workshop that weaves woolens with traditional designs. And there is even a modest Maritime Museum in a house in town; it displays some interesting materials related to the shipbuilding and sailing fleets that were based in Oia (especially during the 19th century). All in all, a stay in Oia can be a restful alternative to other places on Santorini.

Anafi (Anaphe) Island

Some 19 miles east of Santorini (and administratively a subdivision of it) is the small (about 15 square miles) island of Anafi. It has its share of legends, a few ancient ruins, and a monastery, but even a brief side-trip there will be beyond most tourists' capacities. Still, it is described briefly here in case anyone wants to go exploring.

How to Get There

At least one of the scheduled inter-island ships must go from Santorini to Anafi – probably about twice a week. If that weren't convenient, of course, you could hire a boat to take you over; but it should be relatively large – and the sea relatively calm – before you set out.

History of Anafi

Not much is really known about its early history. One classical legend was that when the Argonauts got caught in a storm, Apollo made this small island rise from the sea to provide a refuge. In any case, Apollo was greatly revered here, a temple (see below) being dedicated to him in the Classic age. Throughout most of its history, Anafi's fortunes were linked to Santorini's, even in the great cataclysm c. 1500 B.C. Anafi received the impact of a seismic wave although there is not any evidence of any settlement at this time. And being so small, it was more or less left to go its own way by the Venetians and Turks – although it was the Crispi family (not the Barozzi and Foscoli) who ruled Anafi. In the years 1770-74, however, when the

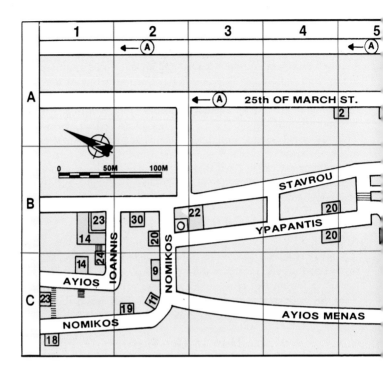

FIRA: TOWN PLAN

To locale points, refer to sequential numbers (before) and the grid-code (after).

A   To Oia (and other points to north)
B   To Skala Fira and port
C   To Akrotiri, Ancient Thera, Kamari, airport, and other points to south

TOURIST SERVICES
1. Foreign Papers & Books (B5)
2. Police Station (A4-5)
3. Post Office (B8)
4. Telephones & Telegrams (B7)
5. Bus Depot (A6)
6. Taxi Stand (A7)
7. Mules/Horses Pick-up Point (C6)
8. Banks (B7)
9. Town Hall (C2)

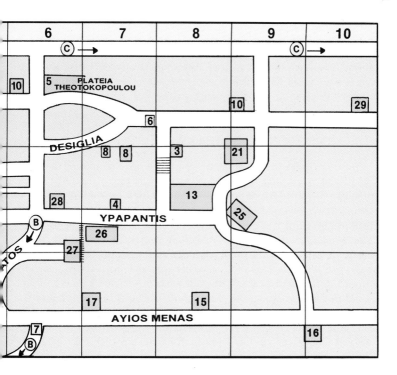

10. Public Toilets (A5) (A9)
11. Cable-car Terminal (C2)
12. Port Police (A5)

CHURCHES

13. Orthodox Cathedral (B8)
14. Roman Catholic Church &
    Convent (B-C1)
15. Ayios Ioannis (C8)
16. Ayios Menas (C10)
17. Ayia Ireni (C7)
18. Ayios Stylianos (C1)

HOMES

19. Ducal House (C2)
20. Private (Modern) Mansions
    (B-2), (B-4)

MUSEUMS & EXHIBITS

21. Prehistoric (including
    Akrotiri) Culture (B9)
22. Historic Culture
    including Ancient Thera) (B3)
23. Chyzis Palace
    (Santorini since the Renais-
    sance) (B1)
24. Rug-making &
    Handicraft School (C1)

HOTELS

25. Hotel Atlantis (B9)
26. Hotel Panorama (B7)
27. Hotel Loukas (B6)
28. Hotel Kavalari (B6)
29. Hotel Kallisti Thira (A10)

Russians undertook to liberate their Greek Orthodox brethren from the Turks, Anafi found that the only thing liberated were some of their antiquities, which showed up in St. Petersburg (Leningrad). (The Russians might have taken more from the Aegean, but other European powers – notably England – had long since carried off many of the movable remains.)

Visiting Anafi

The boat leaves you off at the tiny port of Ayios Nikolaos on the south coast, and from there a 15-minute walk leads up to the only village (population some 300) on the island; known itself as Anafi or Khora, it encircles two sides of a conical hill, on the top of which once stood a castle built by Duke Crispi in the 15th century — little but rubble remains today. The simplest meals and accommodation may be obtained here in this village. A path above the south coast eastward leads (in about $1^1/_2$ hours walk) to Katelimatsa, the site of ancient harbor but now distinguished only by a chapel dedicated to St. Irene; all kinds of remains from the ancient world lie scattered about the promontory while other remains have been incorporated into a shepherd's hut.

Proceeding on another $1^1/_2$ hours along the coast, you come to the site of the old monastery of the Panayia Kalamiotissa ("Our Lady of the Bullrush"); now deserted; its miraculous icon, however, has been placed in a new church built after the earthquake of 1956 and on September 8 the people of Anafi make a pilgrimage here and celebrate the fall festival with traditional dancing. Located on a terrace on a ridge, the rebuilt monastery is on the site of an ancient temple dedicated to Apollo Aigletes ("Radiant Apollo"). The refectory seems to folllow the plan of the temple and its walls and those of other structures here are set with several inscriptions from the Hellenistic period.

Proceeding westward along the ridge toward the center of the island, you would come (after considerable scrambling up some terraced slopes) to the site of the ancient acropolis; all the ancient tombs here were long ago plundered, but many remains of antiquity lie scattered about; down the slope is a chapel with an impressive carved sarcophagus.

Nothing very exciting or significant, then, but an unusual little island for those willing to go this far. And it has been proposed that the famous so-called Strangford Apollo — an Archaic youth, now in the British Museum--came from Anafi.

General Practical Information from A to Z

ALPHABET: See GREEK LANGUAGE

ANTIQUITIES: Greece enforces a very strict law against exporting antiques and antiquites. Anything dating from before 1830 is technically an antique and cannot be exported without official permission. This might be hard to prove in the case of a piece of textile or old jewerly, but the authorities are really interested in stopping the export of such items as ikons or manuscripts. As for genuine antiquities, small items are sold by several legitimate dealers, but permission for export must be obtained: the dealers, should be able to direct you to the proper government office (which has traditionally been at the **National Archaeological Service, Leoforos Vassilissis Sofias 22, Athens).** Be wary of buying anything "under the counter": if it's not genuine, you're being cheated, and if it is genuine you're apt to find yourself in trouble.

AUTOMOBILE CLUB: Greece has a privately supported automobile club or association with offices in all main cities. Its Greek name forms the acronym **ELPA,** by which it is known; it means **Hellenic Touring and Automobile Club.** Its head office is in **Athens** at the **Pyrgos Athinon** (corner of **Vassilissis Sofias** and **Mesogeion Ave).** It can assist you in obtaining an **International Driver's license** (so long as you have a valid license-which in practice is often accepted) or provide advice about insurance or other matters. For its members, **ELPA** provides a range of services, and its emergency repair vehicles will usually stop for any vehicle along the highway.

BABYSITTERS: Greeks have traditionally relied on their "extended families" to perform babysitting, but in recent years-due primarily to the needs of foreigners-Greek women have taken up this chore for money. They are not especially cheap, relative to wages in Greece and elsewhere, but they perform a necessary service. If you need a babysitter, contact the hotel reception desk, the **Tourist Police,** a travel agency, or the **National Tourist Information office.** The higher grade hotels should almost certainly be able to provide someone.

BANKS: There is no shortage of banks in Greek cities. Their normal hours are 8 AM to 2 PM, Monday through Friday, and some open for at least foreign exchange on Saturday mornings, Sunday morning and late afternoon or early evening. But banks do close on the main Greek holidays (See HOLIDAYS), so make sure you do not leave vital transactions to those days. Most goodsized banks maintain separate counters or windows for foreign exchange so be sure you get in the right line. Banks officially- and generally in practice do-give the best exchange rate (and usually give a slightly better rate for travelers' cheques than for foreign currency). If you have bought too many Drachmas and want to buy back your own currency, you must provide the receipts of the Drachma purchases, and even so you will be limited as to how much you can convert back. You may be asked for your passport in any bank transactions, so have it with you. See also MONEY.

BARBERS: There are plenty of barbers in Greece, and you shouldn't need much language to get what you want. It is customary to tip the barber about 10%; if he uses a boy for cleaning up, you give him a few extra Drachma. See also HAIRDRESSERS.

BATHING: See SWIMMING

BICYCLES FOR RENT: Bicycles may be rented-usually from renters of motorbikes, motorscooters, etc. - in the main cities and resort centers. Rates vary, but they obviously become cheaper over longer periods. And if you are planning on renting for a specific trip on a specific occasion, reserve in advance, especially during the main tourist season. See also MOTORBIKES FOR RENT.

BUS TRAVEL: There is frequent public bus service both within all large Greek cities and connecting main cities to smaller villages. In the cities, you pay as you get on the bus at the rear; keep your receipt for possible inspection. For intercity travel, you usually buy the ticket at the starting point; the ticket may include a numbered seat-but Greeks often pay little attention to this. However, especially during the main tourist season, buses can quickly become crowded, so you are advised to buy your ticket as soon as possible. Schedules between main cities and outlying villages have usually been set up for the convenience of villagers who need to come into the city early in the morning and return home late afternoon, so tourists may have to plan around such schedules. If you want to get a bus at a stop along its route, be sure that you signal clearly to the approaching driver, who may not otherwise stop.

CAMPING: Officially there is no longer camping in Greece except at the locales set aside either for government or commercial campsites. The **National Tourist Organization** has a brochure listing all such places around Greece. Such campsites, like those elsewhere, offer a range of support services, from hot water to electric outlets to food. Unofficially, there is still some camping-whether in vehicles or tents-on various beaches and fields. If you do try this, at least respect the property and dispose of all your wastes in approved ways. If you didn't stay too long in one place and picked fairly remote locales, you might get away with such camping.

CAR RENTAL: There are many firms that rent cars-both the well-known international agencies such as **Hertz** and **Avis** and many locally owned firms-in all the large cities and resort centers around Greece. Rates are generally controlled by law, and variations are supposed to reflect different services, etc. The bigger international agencies, for example, can ofer pickups and dropoffs at airports; they are also better equipped to provide quick replacement vehicles should something go wrong. Actual rates vary greatly depending on the size of vehicle, length of time, etc. You will find that it is much easier to rent a car if you have a charge card; otherwise you must leave a large deposit. You will probably want to pay the extra charge for full-coverage coverage insurance (that is, to eliminate any problems with minor damage to the vehicle). You must produce a valid driver's license-in practice, this is accepted without the **International Driver's License.** Do volunteer the names of all individuals who may be driving the vehicle. And during the main tourist season, make your reservation as far in advance as possible.

CHARTER CRUISES: This has become a most popular way of visiting the **Greek islands.** Cruises vary from 2 days to a week or longer, and sometimes include stops at other **Mediterranean ports** (e.g. **Ephesus** or **Constantinople** in **Turkey**). They are not especially cheap, but considering that you save on hotel rooms and have to eat someplace, and that the alternatives (less comfortable small interisland ships or expensive airplanes) do not appeal to many people, these cruises become the best choice for many people. The principal disadvantage is the short time allowed on shore in most cases. Most of these cruises originate in **Athens-Piraeus,** but inquire at any travel agent for information.

CHURCHES: Since about 98% of all Greeks belong to the Greek Orthodox Church, it is not surprising that most churches will be of that faith. Visitors to Greece should make a point of stepping into some of these churches, whether old or new, large or small; best time is when a service is being held-even better when some special holy day or occasion such as a wedding or baptism is being celebrated. (Greeks are happy to see foreigners in attendance). It used to be possible to step into any remote chapel, but with an increase of thefts of ikons and valuables in recent years, many chapels are now kept locked; usually the key is held by the priest or someone else in the nearest village. There are small pockets of **Roman Catholics in Greece** - in the **Ionian, Dodecannese,** and **Cycladic islands,** and of course a large foreign community in Athens - and services are held in their own churches. There are relatively few **Protestants in Greece** and most of these are foreigners in **Athens,** where there are several **Protestant churches.** There are also Jewish synagogues in **Athens** and **Thessaloniki.**

CIGARETTES and CIGARS: Greeks continue to smoke cigarettes as though cancer had never been invented. The Greek cigarettes (and they grow a great deal of tobacco) come in all strengths and prices, and determined smokers should be able to find a brand to substitute for their otherwise very expensive favorites from home. There are limits on how many can be imported free of duty into Greece: 200 cigarettes (300 for citizens of EEC nations), 50 cigars (or 200 grams of tobacco for a pipe).

CLOTHING: If you come during the hot months-May through September-you can get by in most situations with a light wardrobe. Do bring at least a sweater for cool evenings, however. And of course if you intend to spend time at higher elevations, you must bring adequate clothing-for cooler weather, possible rain, and any special requirements (such as rugged shoes for hiking). Greeks are informal dressers, and at beaches almost anything goes; however, they do not like to see people wearing beachwear in towns or in stores away from the beach; villagers are especially conservative, and you will create unnecessary comments if you parade around villages is scanty beachwear. You can always buy needed clothing in Greece, but it is not especially cheap. There are some local specialties, of course-informal shirts, shawls or sweaters, sandals, sunhats, etc.

COMPLAINTS: With literally millions of foreigners moving around Greece each year, it is impossible not to have occasional incidents or cases of dissatisfaction. Many of these arise from language problems or cultural differences. But if you feel you have a legitimate complaint, there are several possibilities. Start with the local **Tourist Police** or **National Tourist Organization office:** the emergency **phone number** for the **Tourist Police** all over Greece is **171. Athens** has a special number for handling complaints by foreigners: **135.** One way to stop possible episodes is to ask for an itemized bill or receipt that you can indicate you intend to show to the **Tourist Police.**

CONSULATES and EMBASSIES: All the major nations of the world maintain embassies in Athens, but most travelers are more apt to need help in some more remote city. Many countries maintain consulates in other Greek cities-and often in unexpected cities, due to levels of commerce or tourism in these areas. Many of these consuls are local nationals, but they are authorized to help. Likewise, even if your own country does not maintain a consulate in a particular city, another country's might be able to help if it primarily a matter-at least at the outset-of finding someone who speaks your language. (Example: You need someone to translate a Greek document).

CREDIT CARDS: The major international and certain national credit cards are accepted in many situations around Greece. The expected scale of acceptance prevails: the more expensive and more internationally-oriented the facility (hotel, restaurant, store), the more likely they are to honor credit cards. You cannot expect small tavernas, little pensions, village shops, to honor such cards. In most cases, those places that honor credit cards display plaques or signs so indicating at the front. And in the case of car rentals, credit cards are actually preferred for they serve to assure the agencies of your credit standing. See also TRAVELERS CHEQUES.

CUSTOMS CONTROL: For the mass of foreigners who visit Greece, customs control is so relaxed that it will hardly be noticed. You will have to pass through passport and customs control on your first point of entry into Greece - for most people, this will mean **Athens, Piraeus,** or one of the border checkpoints at the north, or **Patras.** There are some limits, however, and although you might slip in uninspected, you should know of these. You can bring in unlimited sums of travellers cheques or foreign currency, but you are limited to bringing in 25,000 Drachmas. Limited amount of tobacco products can be brought in; 1 liter of liquor or 1 liter of wine may be imported. Cameras, typewriters, radios, tape-recorders may be brought in as long as they are clearly for personal use; there are some limits on weapons and you should inquire before setting out for Greece. You cannot import explosives or narcotics (or parrots!). In leaving, you are limited to how much olive oil you can take out tax-free (as well as to 10,000 Drachmas and antiques-before 1830-and antiquities without offical permission: See: ANTIQUITIES).

DENTISTS: Dentists are to be found in all large to middle sized cities. Most have trained abroad (and so will speak at least one foreign language) and they will usually have quite modern equipment. Their rates should be quite reasonable. When in need of a dentist, start by asking at the hotel reception desk (especially at the better grade hotels) or the **Tourist Police:** for one thing, someone can then phone ahead and explain your problem.

DOCTORS: Doctors are found in all large to middle-sized cities, although various specialists may be found only in the former. Most of these doctors will have done some of their studies abroad and so will speak at least one foreign language. Their knowledge, equipment, and techniques will be thoroughly up to date. In **Athens** especially, you must expect to pay international rates; elsewhere doctors may be somewhat cheaper. Incidentally, if you had a medical emergency in a small or remote locale, the local people would certainly help in getting a doctor to you or you to a doctor. See also PHARMACIES.

DRIVING IN GREECE: Large numbers of foreigners now drive either their own or rented vehicles around Greece. In both cases you need a **valid driver's licence,** and theoretically you should have an **International Driver's Licence.** It if it is your own car you are bringing into Greece, you need its registration (or log book) and you need proof of adequate insurance. There will be limits (usually about 4 months) on the length of time you can drive your car in Greece; you can usually get an extension (for 8 months) to continue driving your car without any major registration fees. The car will be entered in your passport, so if you were for any reason want to sell it in Greece, you must make very sure you are in full compliance with Greek laws governing such transactions.

Your car-and all rented vehicles - are exempt from the Greek law governing alternate Sunday regulations (even number plates-odd number plates). But foreigners must obey speed limits (and police can demand payment of fines on the spot) and you should observe parking regulations: the Greek custom is for police to remove license plates-and then force you to go around to a police station to pay the fine to get your plates back!

Fuel of all grades is available all over Greece-at some of the highest rates in the world. Because almost all Greeks drive imported cars (some foreign vehicles are now being assembled in Greece), there is no problem obtaining spare parts or experienced repairmen for your vehicle. (You may be amazed at the age of some of the boys who work on your vehiche-under adult supervision you hope).

Driving is on the right. Roads are not always well marked for danger spots or unusual conditions: curves, soft shoulders, fallen rocks, steep gradients-these are often not indicated. And although Greece has built up an impressive national highway system, many roads are in need of basic maintenance: it is not uncommon to encounter major potholes or rough stretches in the middle of otherwise decent highways. In addition, Greek drivers themselves retain a few habits from the days before motor vehicles were so common: they turn into main highways, stop along the road without warning, weave in and out in city streets. (Greece has one of the highest fatality rates from driving accidents). But with basic caution, you should have no trouble driving in Greece.

DRUGS: Greek authorities take a very strict approach on importing drugs. On the other hand, Greek men in certain locales do smoke marijuana and use even stronger drugs. But foreigners would be advised to have nothing to do with drugs while in Greece.

DRYCLEANING: There are plenty of drycleaning establishments in all large to medium-sized cities. It is relatively cheap and fast-you should be able to get your clothing back within the day if you bring it early and make your needs clear. See also LAUNDRY.

EARTHQUAKES: Despite the publicity that attends earthquakes in Greece-from the days of **Lost Atlantis** to the ones that struck the **Athens area** in 1980 - these need not be of concern to visitors. The odds are that the most anyone will experience might be a slight tremor. One might just as well stay away from **Italy**-or **California,** for that matter.

EASTER: In many respects, **Easter** is the major occasion of the Greek year. Many Foreigners deliberately time their visit to Greece so as to be able to experience some of the events associated with the **Greek Easter.** Because it does not usually coincide with the **Easter** celebrated in the **Western Christian churches,** care must be taken that you do not arrive at the wrong time. The **Greek Orthodox Easter** is calculated as follows: it must fall after the first full moon following the first day of spring, (as is true with **Western Christian Easter)** but it must also fall after the **Jewish Passover.** This then affects the **Lent** period-including the two weeks before **Lent** known as Carnival, with its festivities and parades, culminating in **Clean Monday**, with its vegetarian feast and kit-flying. And of course **Good Friday** depends on Easter's date: this is marked by a funeral procession through the streets. Saturday evening involves a church service that ends at midnight with the lighting of candles. **Easter Sunday** itself is an occasion for feasting and festivities. And even the Monday after is observed as a holiday. Ideally you should try to get invited to some village where the traditional **Easter** is observed, but even in the large cities there is enough to make a stranger feel the full impact of Easter on Greeks.

ELECTRICITY: Greece has now converted to (A ternating Current) at 220 voltage. This means that **Americans** must have converters for their 110-115 volt electrical appliances. Furthermore Greek outlets and plugs vary considerably from both **American** and many **European** standard types, so converters may be required. But electricity is virtually everywhere in Greece.

EMBASSIES: See CONSULATES AND EMBASSIES

EMERGENCIES: For emergency help of any kind, you will get a response 24 hours a day (and hopefully in a language you can speak) by dialing either the **Tourist Police (171)** or the regular police, **(100)** anywhere in Greece. (However, in smaller towns and villages, you will first have to dial the code to the nearest large city). Another possibility is to get to a hotel's reception desk and ask them to make the first call.

FISHING: There is relatively little freshwater fishing in most parts of Greece-and the saltwater fishing in the Mediterranean is not as good as one might assume. But Greeks do catch fish, obviously. No licence is required. Nor is any licence is required. Nor is any license required for underwater speargun fishing: however, you must be at least 200 meters (667 feet) away from any other people in the water.

FOOD AND DRINK: Whatever else people come to Greece to enjoy, they all spend a fair amount of their time in eating and drinking. And since food and drink end up being among the main ingredients-and usually pleasures-of a Greek holiday, certain things might be said to improve their chances of being enjoyed.

To start with the first meal, breakfast-in most hotels this will be the "continental" type: coffee, possibly some sort of juice, bread, butter, and jelly. Unfortunated, all too often these are less than exciting. If you are required to take breakfast as part of your hotel's rates, that's that. But if you have a choice, you might consider going out and assembling your own breakfast: buying fresh fruit, buying your own roll or cheese pie or sweet, and then taking nothing but coffee in a cafe. Depending on your personal preference, you can take your large dinner at noon or in the evening, as most Greek restaurants offer the same menu, noon and night. (Only the more luxurious restaurants prepare a more elaborate menu for the evening). But consider: if you intend to move about in the heat of the afternoon, you should probably eat light. Then treat yourself to something refreshing late afternoon. For Greeks eat their evening meal late-anything before 8 PM is considered early. Another variation is to assemble your own picnic for the noon meal-fresh fruits, bread, cheeses, sliced meats or sardines, etc. And when ordering meals in restaurants, you are welcome to go back to the kitchen area to inspect and point out exactly what you want (and don't hesitate to send back anything that is not what you want). If you do not care for much olive oil, indicate that you want little or no **ladhi**. And if you find the food tepid to cold, indicate that you want your food served **zestós**. (If you're lucky, they'll get it as hot as you prefer it).

Greeks like to eat snacks when drinking anything alcoholic. Shrimp, tomato slices, bits of cheese, artichoke leaves - these are known as **mezés** or **mezedákis;** similar hors d'oeuvres as part of a full meal are **orektiká. Mezés** can be had at almost any little cafe or snack place. Sweets and ice cream **(pagotá)** are obtained at special sweetshops and cafés. Traditionally Greeks go to these places for desserts, which are not available at typical restaurant.

Coffee was not traditionally served at restaurants, either, but now, to satisfy their many foreign patrons, some restaurants have taken to serving coffee. You must specify whether you want **ellenikós kafés** or "American" (or "French") coffee; the latter will usually be powdered coffee, while the former is what is widely known abroad as the Turkish style-a small cup with the muddy coffee taking up about the bottom third of the cup. The sugar is boiled with the coffee and you must specify the degree of sweetness you want: medium is **métrios,** sweet in **glykó,** light is **me olighi,** and no sugar at all is **skétos.** Tea is available, too. And Greeks usually take a glass of cold water with everything they eat or drink. Beer is a popular drink-there are several brands brewed in Greece that are quite decent. As for wines, the native Greek wines certainly can't compete with the world's better varieties, but some are adequate. There is first of all a choice between the **retsina** - wines that have been stored in "resinated" barrels and thus have a mild turpentine(!) flavor: not to everyone's taste, but in fact they go well with the Greek menu-and the **aretsinoto** wines. In addition to the usual whites, pinks, and reds, there are sweet dessert wines and quite good Greek brandies. There is also the Greek **oúzo,** made from distilling the crushed mash after the juice has been pressed from the grapes and then adding a slight anisette flavor.

Above all, whether eating or drinking, in fancy restaurants or simple tavernas, everyone should occasionally experiment with some of the different items on the Greek menu. Don't stay in the rut with the same **moussaká** and Greek salad.

See also RESTAURANTS. And for a discussion of special foods and drinks, see pages 91-92.

GREEK LANGUAGE: The Greek language is far too complex and subtle to even begin to be taught or learned in a book like this. But there are a few basics that can be conveyed. Elsewhere a short list of words and phrases are provided to help the traveler in the more common situations.

The Written language: Most visitors to Greece will have little to do with written Greek except to attempt to read signs, menus, etc. Greek pronunciation is difficult enough so that its finer points could involve long discussions. Here is the alphabet with the English equivalent of the most common sounds so that at least a start can be made on reading Greek.

The Spoken language: Acquiring even the most basic spoken Greek is difficult or not, depending on an individual's skill in picking up a foreign language. But because of the unfamiliar alphabet, many foreigners get easily discouraged: there is not that gratuitous gain that comes from just looking at words in some foreign languages and gradually realizing that you can figure out meanings. Yet anyone should be able to rely on their ear and then try to approximate pronunciations. Greeks are genuinely appreciative of any such efforts. One problem, however, that Greeks have ignoring: their language depends so much on the accent's falling on the precise syllable that this becomes at least as important as the purity of the sound. When in doubt, try shifting the accent until you hit the proper syllable.

The casual traveler need not become concerned about the historical rivalries between the "pure" and demotic spoken Greek: the demotic will be fine for all situations. Likewise, although there are numerous dialects spoken in various parts of Greece-some quite different in pronunciation and vocabulary-the foreigner will be doing fine just to speak a basic Greek. Put another way, dialect variations are the least of a foreigner's problems!

AND INTERPRETERS: Officially licensed guides can be provided from the **National Tourist Organization offices** or by the bigger travel agents. Their fees are also officially controlled-and depend on such factors as the time involved, the number in the party, the difficulty of the excursion, etc. Tours organized by travel agencies, of course, usually provide guides who speak the language(s) of the majority of the foreigners taking the tour. If you are lucky, you will get a guide who not only is comfortable with your language but has a true command of the subject-that is, you will get much more than a mechanical-rote recitation of facts.

HAIRDRESSERS: There are many hairdressers in all large to medium-sized Greek cities. You can get a complete line of services. Tipping is expected-perhaps 10% for the principal hairdresser, half that for the assistant.

HITCHHIKING: As long as basic precautions are observed, hitchhiking (also known to Europeans as "autostop") is generally allowed throughout Greece. Young women, whether alone or in pairs, should exercise special judgment as to the rides they accept.

HOLIDAYS: There are two types of holidays that tourists will want to know about while in Greece. One includes the national holidays when not only all banks, museums, archaeological sites, almost all stores, and even many restaurants are closed. These are the following days:

January 1-	New Year's day
January 6-	Epiphany
Last Monday before Lent	
Good Friday	Movable dates (See EASTER)
Easter Sunday	
Easter Monday	
March 25	Greek Independence Day
May 1	Spring Festival, or May Day
August 15-	Assumption of the Virgin Mary
October 28-	Okhi (No!) Day (Second World War incident)
December 25-	Christmas Day

But it addition to these national holidays, there are numerous local holidays and festivals-in honor of some historical or patriotic event, a saint, an age-old festival. In particular, "name-days" are major occasions when the saint's name is one of the more popular ones: people with that name often come from great distances to a monastery, chapel, or village where that saint is especially honored. Sometimes Greek festivities go on for two or more days, involving dancing and feasting. Foreigners are traditionally welcomed, and anyone with a taste for such occasions should inquire from the **National Tourist Organization office** or **Tourist Police** - or, for that matter, from almost any Greek who seems informed-about any forthcoming holiday of this kind. See also HOURS, EASTER.

HOSPITALITY: Greek hospitality is legendary, and it usually lives up to its reputation, especially in more remote villages and where only a few foreigners are involved. But in recent years, with the influx of literally millions of foreigners annually, there has inevitably been some pulling back: there is no way that Greeks can "relate to" every single foreigner who crosses paths with them, let alone afford to extend the full panoply of traditional hospitality. However, arrive in a small party in a remote village and you may still be treated as a special guest-offered special drinks and food, presented with little gifts when you leave. Greek males still usually insist on paying for meals when they take a foreigner to a favorite eating place. You will often be offered a coffee or cold drink when visiting with a Greek-and the Greeks present will expect you to accept even as they refuse anything for themselves. But this hospitality works both ways. Greeks in these situations will often question foreigners about fairly personal matters-why a married couple doesn't have children, how much money you have paid for certain items. And once the preliminaries are underway, Greeks expect you to participate to the end: if they have begun to plan a meal for you, they would be genuinely hurt if you ran off to save them the trouble and expense. So don't embark on these encounters unless you are prepared to enjoy them all the way.

HOSPITALS: All large, medium-sized, and even some quite small towns have hospitals or at least clinics. You might go direct to one if you have some medical emergency. Only in the larger cities, of course, could you expect to find a full range of services and specialists. Greek hospitals provide minimal nursing care: a member of the family will often bed down next to the patient to provide full attention, meals, etc. Most foreigners will never have any contact with hospitals, but if you had to you will find that they are quite adequate. See also DOCTORS, EMERGENCIES.

HOSTELS: There are **Youth Hostels** throughout Greece - in most major cities and also in tourist centers. You will almost certainly be asked to produce a membership card from a recognized Youth Hostel association; if you do not have one from your home country, you can join (for a fee) the **Greek Youth Hostels Association** (at 4 Dragatsaniou Street, Athens). There is usually a limit of 5 days on your stay at these hostels.

HOTELS: There are hotels to suit all tastes and all pocketbooks all over Greece. If you have particular preferences as to price, location, or other specifics, you should reserve in advance for the main tourist season: no one ever spends the night on the street, but you cannot be certain of getting the exact hotel you want. At other times of the year, however, there is generally a surplus of beds. All hotel and room accommodations in Greece are quite strictly controlled-as to price, conditions, etc.-by the government. There are various classes or categories, of hotels, form Deluxe and then Class A through E; the criteria may not always seem important to all guests (e.g. size of public rooms, telephones in rooms), but in general the categories reflect the levels of amenities. Many tourists find the Class C hotels-most of which are relatively new-quite adequate (and they cost about one-half a Class A hotel and two-thirds a Class B). The prices are supposed to be posted in each room, but sometimes it is hard for a hotel to keep up with all seasonal changes.

Ask for the price of the room before you agree to anything (and then ask to inspect it, if you care to). Find out if the price quoted includes all taxes and whether it includes any meals: hotels are allowed to require clients to take breakfast, if offered by the hotel, and the Class B, A, and Deluxe hotels may also require clients to take at least one other meal if the hotel maintains a dining room. Service charges should be included in the price quoted, but you may want to tip a bit extra anyone who has done you any personal favors. Prices may be raised during the "high" tourist season (and may be lowered during the off season); hotels can also charge an extra 10% if you stay less than three nights. It all sounds quite complicated, but in practice you are told a price of a room and that's usually the end of it. Do clarify the various possibilities, however, if you are concerned.

HOURS: Greek shop hours can be a quite complicated subject, but in general stores open at 8AM and close around 1:30 or 2 PM, Monday through Saturday; on several days a week (but not Saturday) some shops reopen again from about 5 to 8:30 PM. Inquire in the morning if you have any special needs for that day. And of course all shops observe the national holidays. See HOLIDAYS.

HUNTING: Foreigners may hunt within Greece but only with a license and with limitations on seasons, type of game, etc. There are also limits on the types of weapons and ammunition you can bring in. Inquire at the **National Tourist Organization** or a **Greek Embassy** abroad if this is to be an important part of your visit to Greece.

INFORMATION: There are various sources for detailed information about Greece. Abroad, there are the **Greek Embassies** and **Consulates;** the **National Tourist Organization** maintains offices in many of the principal cities of the world; and travel agents have some types of touristic information. Within Greece, there are the various offices of the **National Tourist Organization,** the **Tourist Police,** and also the travel agencies. One of the problems for all of these offices is to keep up with the many changes from year to year and from season to season in schedules, prices, etc. Thus, not until you actually get to Greece can you probably find out exact times and costs of the sailings to the many Greek islands; what you should be able to learn while still abroad is whether such service is usually available.

LAUNDRY: Laundry can usually be placed at a drycleaning establishment to be picked up within 24 hours, and the better class hotels usually will take care of laundry for their clients. But wherever it is done, it will seem expensive (especially relative to so many other costs in Greece). But every item will be neatly ironed, and in some situations this service may be a necessary expense. There are self-service laundries in only a few large cities there has been one in the **Plaka** section of **Athens.** Most tourists simply make do by washing out things in their rooms and then hanging them on the usually present balcony.

LUGGAGE: Greek air terminals and bus stations usually do not provide any place to leave luggage for even short periods of time. Tourists are left to make their own arrangements-with a cafe, restaurant, hotel, store, or wherever. Offer a reasonable sum for the service, and although it cannot be legally guaranteed, your luggage should always be safe.

MEDICINES: See PHARMACIES

MENU: See RESTAURANTS

MONEY: The basic Greek currency is the Drachma. The Lepta-100 make up a Drachma-has all but vanished from common usage, although occasionally prices are quoted with a 50 Lepta. (When Greek shopkeepers or others lack small change, they automatically "round off"-sometimes to your advantage, sometimes to theirs). The exchange rate of the Drachma with various foreign currencies has been fluctuating so in recent years that it would be misleading to provide specific figures here. As soon as you find out the exchange rate for your own national currency, calculate some basic equivalencies-that is, what does 5 Drachmas, equal, 10 Drachmas, 50

Drachmas, etc. This will provide a general sense of what things are costing. Technically you are limited to importing 25,000 Drachmas in currency; most foreigners are never even questioned, let alone inspected, but there is no real "black market" in Greek currency and little opportunity for most people to gain anything by violating the law. See also BANKS.

MOTORBIKES FOR RENT: Motorbikes may be rented from various agents in the main cities and resort centers. Rates vary but they obviously become cheaper over longer periods. During the main tourist season and over holidays, you should probably reserve in advance. To rent a motorbike, however, you must be at least 18 years of age and licensed to operate one. You (and any passengers) must wear a protective helmet. And you should carry all the insurance you can get. See also BICYCLES FOR RENT.

MOUNTAINEERING: It may be overlooked-considering that most people come to Greece to enjoy the beaches and water-that Greece also has many fine mountains that offer challenging and enjoy-able possibilities. There is a **Greek Mountainclimbing Club** (EOS is the Greek acronym), with branches in many cities, and foreigners are made to feel welcome on their excursions and in their facilities. They maintain various huts on major mountains. Although the peaks may not seem that high by world standards, the weather conditions often make some of the ascents quite difficult, and certainly no one should set out to climb unless properly equipped and experienced. Consult the **National Tourist Organization** for details about contacting a local mountaineering club or obtaining a local guide.

MOVIES: No one would ever travel to Greece to see a movie-the selection, even in **Athens,** is usually dismal, and in smaller cities it is hard to know where such movies have come from. But there are times when someone might want to retreat to a movie, and during the summer, when there are many outdoor movie theaters, it can be quite pleasant to sit under the starry Mediterranean sky and sit back and enjoy a movie you'd feel guilty about seeing at home. Most foreign films in Greece are shown in their original language and with Greek subtitles, but ask to make sure before you enter.

NEWSPAPERS AND MAGAZINES: There is a large selection of foreign-language (that is, non-Greek) newspapers and magazines to be found in the large and medium-sized cities and also in all tourist centers.

Athens has an English-language daily, **The Athens News,** and a fine English-language monthly, **The Athenian.** There is also a good selection of papers and periodicals brought in from abroad; they tend to be expensive (compared to prices at home) and the news will seem a bit dated (when you first arrive), but the longer you stay the more you may appreciate these links with the world.

PARKING: There was once a time when there were so few cars that finding a parking place was no problem in Greece. Then came a phase when the car population "exploded" so fast they took over every available sidewalk and corner. Now the Greek police have begun to fight back: in Athens and some cities, the police remove the license plates when your car is in violation and you must go to the local stationhouse and pay the fine to retrieve your plates. Meters are appearing in some cities. Parking restrictions are generally enforced, for foreigners as well as Greeks. Athens and several other cities and tourist centers have set aside a few places for tourist parking (marked by signs) but during the main season these are as hard, to find free as any other places.

PASSPORTS AND VISAS: A valid national passport is all that is required of most visitors to Greece-although you will probably be asked to fill out an entry card on the airplane or ship-so long as you are a transient: This period varies (depending on reciprocal arrangements with the individual's home country), but for **British** and **Commonwealth** subjects this is three months and for **Americans,** two months. For longer stays visas must be applied for: Inquire at the **Tourist Police** or **National Tourist Organization** as to how to proceed.

PENSIONS: These are a cheaper, more basic type of accommodation to be found in locales where a lot of travelers pass through. You probably won't have a private toilet or bath, and the buildings will usually be older, but linen will be clean and some people prefer the more homey atmosphere. Breakfast is usually available at a pension. Sea also ROOMS TO RENT.

PHARMACIES: Pharmacies, drugstores, or chemists, there are plenty of them around Greece and they carry a fairly full selection of prescription drugs as well as general health, sanitary, and cosmetic items. (A pharmacy is usually clearly marked by a **red Maltese cross**). There will always be at least one pharmacy open, 24 hours a day, in any large city: the closed ones should have a sign in their window indicating which one is open. If you have special medical needs, of course, you had better make arrangements with you own doctor at home before setting off.

PHOTOGRAPHY: Greece is famed as a photographer's paradise, what with its light and subjects. There are plenty of shops selling films and camera supplies-but all are expensive and you are advised to bring your own. You can get your films developed in relatively short times. In traveling about Greece, be careful to observe the occasional restrictions against photographing in areas of military bases.

POLICE: See EMERGENCIES

POST OFFICE: Any good sized city will have its post offices, and larger cities will have several branch office. They keep varied hours, but best is to get there in the morning. Some will open for only limited service in the late afternoon-postage stamps or for **Poste Restante**. (This latter refers to mail addressed to someone with no other known or fixed address-what Americans known as **General Delivery**). Postage rates vary considerably (and rise inevitably) depending on the nature of the item (post card, letter, etc.), the weight, the destination, etc. The best is to know the basic stamps for most of your mail (that is, air mail post cards to your homeland, the lightest air mail letters, etc.) and be prepared to have any mail in question weighed. Stamps can often be purchased at certain stationery shops but you will pay a slight surcharge for the privilage.

PRICES: The one thing certain is that they will rise over time, in Greece as elsewhere. Some prices, however, do come down during the off-season-hotels in particular. By and large, prices are well marked for most items you will be purchasing, whether food in the market, or clothes in a store, and Greeks do not appreciate your trying to negotiate prices. If a shopkeeper sees you about to leave he may make some kind of a reduction or offer, but he does not want you to turn every purchase into a bazaar haggling.

RADIO: There are several possibilities for foreigners who like to keep up with the news via radio and in their own language. Greek stations provide at least one brief program daily with news and weather in **English French,** and **German.** The American Armed Forces **Radio** broadcasts 24 hours daily, with frequent news updates. And there is the **BBC** overseas and the **Voice of America.**

REDUCTIONS: There are some reductions in admissions to museums and archaeological sites but they are limited to special groups. Foreign students of subjects directly related to the world of Greek art and archaeology can get a pass that allows for a 50% reduction to all national sites and museums (not to locally run). Students who present an

International Student Identity Card are granted a reduced fee at some places. And a very special group of archaeologists, professors of art and architecture and classical subjects, museum professionals, **UNESCO** and some other government officials are given free entry to sites and museums. If you think you qualify, go to the **Directorate of Antiquities,** 14 Aristidou St., Athens, with proper identification and find out how to comply.

RELIGION: See CHURCHES

RESTAURANTS: There is no problem in finding a restaurant in Greece, and although they range from the quite elaborate and expensive to the rather dingy and cheap, most foreigners end up patronizing a relatively narrow spectrum. They are officially classed, and this affects the prices they are allowed to charge. The easy way to approach a restaurant is to make sure its appearance appeals and then look at some standard item on the menu which should always be posted out front-and see how its price compares with the same item in other places you've eaten in. Not necessarily, but usually, if the moussaka or Greek salad is expensive, then everything will be expensive. Once you have decided to eat there, go to the kichen area and select your foods-most proprietors are happy to have you do so; this eliminates the need for a lot of talking and the possibility of some unwanted surprises. Send back food if it is not what you want. The standard printed Greek menu has its prices listed in two columns; that on the left is the price before the obligatory service charge, that on the right includes the service percentage-and it is the latter you will be billed for. It is customary, even so, to tell the waiter to keep a small extra sum when he presents the change; and if there was a "waterboy" for your table you leave a few Drachmas for him.

ROOMS TO RENT: In some of the more crowded tourist centers individual families have taken to renting rooms in their homes. They are supposed to be supervised so that basic sanitary practices are observed, no matter how simple the accommodation. They are relatively cheap and many people find such rooms adequate. See also PENSIONS.

SAILING: See YACHTS

SHOESHINE: In the larger cities, young boys or even men will be shining shoes in various public areas. Agree on the price beforehand-and if you are in doubt, ask a Greek to help establish the cost. A small tip is customary.

SHOPPING AND SOUVENIRS: In the largest and even in relatively small cities of Greece, you will be able to purchase almost any item you need for your stay in Greece. Often as not it will even be your favorite brand, since Greeks import virtually everything: your favorite suntan lotion, your preferred instant coffee-they'll probably be available. But these are not what most people come to Greece to buy. It is the souvenirs and specialties of Greece that interest most travelers, and here the selection, is almost overwhelming, especially in the major tourist centers. Since everyone's taste differs as to what constitutes a suitable souvenir there is no use laying down rules. Take your time and look around: it is not that shops cheat but simply that prices often will be lower in one place than another-and sometimes the lowest price will be in some unexpected location. (Even then, the difference may be relatively few Drachmas, so you must ask yourself how much of your limited time you want to spend in comparison shopping). It is difficult to find genuine handmade artifacts, but they are available, and often not that much more expensive than the massproduced items. Often it is the smaller and less centrally located shops that have the unusual items, so leave the main streets lined with gift shops and go looking. Even then, don't give too much credence to claims of age or uniqueness or "the last one left...": just buy what you like at the price you feel you want to pay See also **PRICES** and HOURS.

SPORTS: Those who like to include active sports in their vacations and travels will find many opportunities to do so in Greece. In the winter, for instance, there are several ski lifts operating (most of them in central and northern Greece, but one in the White Mountains of Crete). There are several gold clubs in Greece (near Athens, and on **Rhodes** and **Corfu**). There is horseback riding (at Athens, Salonica, and on Crete). Several of the major resort hotels offer waterskiing, and many public beaches now have paddleboats and surfsails for rent. And Greek youths can usually be found playing informal games of soccer (football) or basket-ball: if you ask, you could probably join in. See also MOUNTAINEERING, SWIMMING, TENNIS, UNDERWATER SPORTS, YACHTING.

SWIMMING: Swimming-or at least sunbathing is perhaps the main attraction for many visitors to Greece, and there are almost limitless beaches. In fact, though, not all Greek beaches are as sandy as you might wish. Inquire if you have a strong preference and a choice as to where the sandy beach is located. Likewise, not all beaches are as clean as you might wish although if you get away from a city or built-up area the water should be perfectly clean and clear. What you cannot always escape-anywhere in the Mediterranean - is the tar that washes ashore and gets into the sand: a beach may look perfectly clean, but as you walk along the sand your feet pick up the buried tar. (This is one reason many people have taken to bringing flexible mats to the beaches: to save their towels from getting fouled). The usual precautions about avoiding undertows and unexpected currents should be observed. Many cities operate public beach facilities-changing rooms, showers, etc. Although women go topless on many Greek beaches, nudist beaches are officially forbidden and in some areas local individuals actively seek to enforce the ban; in some places, if it is done with discretion, it will be ignored. Lastly the Mediterranean is not the tropics, and most people find the swimming season lasts only from May through September.

TAXIS: Taxis remain relatively cheap in Greece. They can also be hard to hire during certain busy hours-and for that reason, Greeks often share taxis, each party paying the metered fare to their destination. There is a minimum fare, too-no matter how short the distance. There may also be some surcharges beyond the metered fare: for night rides, for certtain holidays, for luggage, to airports, etc. (Drivers should be able to indicate any such surcharges). If it is to be an especially long trip, negotiate the fee before leaving. If it is to a remote locale and you want the driver to wait, there are set fees for waiting time. With two or more individuals sharing the cost, a taxi offers a reasonable way to make best use of a limited time in Greece.

TELEPHONES AND TELEGRAMS: In a few large cities, it has been traditional to use the phones available at many kiosks (or **peripterons**); you dial first and after you have completed your call you pay the proprietor. Now a large red telephone is replacing this system-and you must insert the coin first (it has for some time been a two-Drachma coin). Increasingly, too, phone booths are appearing all over Greece, and for these you need a two - Drachma coin. In some special phone booths you can even dial long distance, but most foreigners (as do most Greeks) will prefer to go to the office of the national phone company **(OTE)** and use the attended services. If you know-or can learn-the code numbers for your desired call, you can dial direct to virtually any place in the world. (Be persistent, though: the Greek phone system is good, but you must often try dialing several times to make your connection). When you are finished with your call, you step over to the attendant who will read the meter and provide you with a ''bill'' Since many Greeks still do not have telephones, these offices can be quite crowded at certain times, so go well in advance if you must place a call within a set period. Telegrams are sent from these same offices. The forms are printed in English as well as Greek, and the attendants are usually adept at dealing with foreigners' queries. Large hotels might be able to help you, too, with any special problems.

TENNIS: There are a fair number of tennis courts around Greece and most are open to non-Greeks (and non-members of the sponsoring clus). Naturally the courts tend to be concentrated in a few areas-Athens (and its nearby beach resorts), large cities such as **Salonika** and **Patras** and in the more popular holiday centers such as Crete, Rhodes, and Corfu. Inquire at offices of the **National Tourist Organization** for details; if tennis is a vital part of your holiday in Greece, you should make certain of arrangements before going to a particular locale.

THEFT: This is virtually a non-existent problem in Greece. Luggage can be left unattended almost anywhere, purses or cameras can be forgotten - at a restaurant - you will always find them waiting for you. On the other hand, it would be silly to leave a lot of currency or small valuables (jewels watches, etc.) lying around in your hotel room: there are simply too many people passing through.

TIME: Greece is two hours ahead of **Greenwich Mean Time** (that is, **London's** time). Greece now observes **Summer Time** (in which clocks are set one hour ahead) on the same schedule as its fellow **Common Market** members. As for time during the Greek day, Greeks do not concern themselves much with punctuality. Beyond that, when they say "tomorrow morning", they may mean at 12 noon; "this afternoon" may well mean 4 PM. Make a fixed appointment, by all means, but do not get excited if it isn't kept to the minute.

TIPPING: Greeks used to consider it as beneath their dignity to accept tips, but the influx of foreign tourists has changed all that. Even so by including the service charges in restaurant bills and hotel bills, Greeks try to eliminate some of the awkwardness involved in tipping. It is customary to give the waiter at least some "rounded off" change (e.g. the 15 Drachmas over a 385 Drachma bill); coins left on the table will go to the waterboy if there has been one. If you have had some personal contact or asked special services of personnel in your hotel, it is certainly not out of line to present a tip. Barbers, hairdressers, shoe-shiners, and ushers (in movies as well as theaters) traditionally get modest tips. Taxi drivers are not supposed to expect tips, but you can expect a less than gracious smile if you do not at least give a small sum over the fare.

TOILETS: Hotels that most foreigners now stay in have modern toilet facilities (although the plumbing may look a bit exotic). Many of the older restaurants and tavernas, however, have quite primitive toilets: if you are squeamish about this, use your hotel toilet before going out to eat. There are public toilets (the attendants expect a tip) in all medium sized to large Greek cities-but they are often fairly primitive, too. Most of the better hotels have separate toilet facilities for their patrons, and if you look as though you belong you can usually make use of them.

TRAVELERS CHEQUES: All the better known travelers cheques are honored in banks, hotels, restaurants that cater to foreigners, and tourist gift shops. Do not expect every little corner store or village taverna, however, to accept a travelers cheque: buy your Drachmas before setting off for the countryside. See also CREDIT CARDS and BANKS.

UNDERWATER SPORTS: SCUBA diving is generally forbidden in Greek waters-the exception being in certain areas and under some supervision. (This restriction is because the Greeks fear that too many divers could lead to losses of their antiquities still to be found around the coasts.) Inquire at the National Tourist Organization for specifics. However, snorkeling (that is, with just a breathing tube, mask, and flippers) is allowed (as is fishing with a speargun, so long as it is not close to swimmers: See FISHING).

VILLAS FOR RENT: It is relatively easy-if expensive! to rent completely furnished villas in many of the more popular holiday locales around Greece. (Villas, by the way, are distinguished from "houses" in that the former usually are out of the main residential areas and usually have a bit of land). Many villas are now rented only through various travel agents or firms specializing in such rentals: inquire of the National Tourist Organization or of major travel agents. Villas can be very expensive during the main season, but if several people are sharing the cost and make a fair number of meals at home, a villa can end up being relatively cheap.

VISAS: See PASSPORTS AND VISAS

WATER: The water of Greece is safe to drink in virtually any place the average traveler will be. (If foreigners sometimes complain of minor stomach ailments when traveling in Greece, it probably is not the water; in any case, it way be little more than a shift from one water to another-the type of upset one could experience in moving from any city to another). The fresh cold water from a natural spring is one of the delights of Greece. If you are truly sensitive, of course, you can always drink bottled water. A more realistic problem might be to get hot water whenever you want it in your hotel: ask beforehand to find out if hot water is provided at only certain hours.

YACHTING: There are numerous firms that rent yachts-mostly with crews-and this has become a popular way to tour Greece. They are undoubtedly expensive at first hearing, but if the cost is divided among several people, and then hotels, other transportation, and at least some meals are being eliminated, the end result is not that expensive. These yachts come in all sizes, with or without sail, and with greater or lesser degrees of luxury. Inquire of the National Tourist Organization or major travel agents for more details.

YOUTH HOSTELS: SEE HOSTELS

ZOOS: For those people who like to round out their view of a foreign land by visiting the local zoo, Greece offers nothing truly worthy of that name. Athens, however, does have a modest display of animals in the National Garden, and it offers the advantage of being central and a convenient retreat from the heat and bustle of the city. And many Greek cities maintain small collections of animals in their public parks-often including some of the less familiar species of Greece such as the famous wild goat of Crete. Inquire of the local **Tourist Police** if you enjoy such diversions.

A little Greek for travelers

A α (álfa)	As in far.
Β β (víta)	Closer to a soft v than to b.
Γ γ (gámma)	Before a, o, u: **gh.**
	Before e, i: **y.**
Δ δ (dhélta)	Closer to **dh** than
	to hard **d.**
E ε (épsilon)	As in sell.
Z ζ (zíta)	As in zeal.
H η (íta)	As in machine.

Θ θ (thíta)	As in **th**eater.
Ι ι (jóta)	As in mach**i**ne.
Κ κ (káppa)	As in **k**it.
Λ λ (lámdha)	As in **l**amp.
Μ μ (mí)	As in **m**it.
Ν ν (ní)	As in **n**ot.
Ξ ξ (xí)	As **ks** sound (as in e**x**tra)
Ο ο (ómikron)	As in **o**ar.
Π π (pí)	As in **p**it.
Ρ ρ (ró)	As in **r**ed.
Σ σ ς (síghma)	As in **s**it.
Τ τ (táf)	As in **t**ap.
Υ υ (ípsilon)	As in mach**i**ne.
Φ φ (fí)	As in **f**ish.
Χ χ (chí)	A **kh** sound (as in **Khan).**
Ψ ψ (psí)	A **ps** sound (as in a**ps**e)
Ω ω (oméga)	As in **o**de.

BASIC DAILY SITUATIONS

Yes	né
Yes indeed!	málista
No	óchi
Greetings!	chérete!
Good morning	kaliméra
Good evening	kalispéra
Good night	kaliníkta
Stay well!	sto kaló
Excuse me	me sinchoríte **or** signómi!
Please	parakaló
Thank you	efcharistó
Not at all	típota
How are you	Ti kánete? **or** pos páte?
Very well	polí kalá
Do you speak English?	Miláte angliká?
I don't understand	Dhen katalavéno
What is that called?	Pos to léne aftó?

How do you say that in Greek?	Pos to léne aftó? sta ellhniká?
What is your name?	Pos sas léne?
My name is-	Me léne-
Mister	kírios
Mrs.	kiría
Child	pedhi
Much	polí
Little	lígho
Over	epáno
Under	káto
There	ekí
Here	edó
Big	megálos
Little	mikrós

NUMBERS

1	éna	18	dhekaoktó
2	dhío	19	dhekaenéa
3	tría	20	íkossi
4	téssara	21	íkosiéna
5	pénte	30	triánda
6	éxi	40	saránda
7	eftá	50	penínda
8	októ	60	exínda
9	enéa	70	evdomínta
10	dhéka	80	ogdhónda
11	éndheka	90	enenínda
12	dódheka	100	ekató
13	dhekatría	200	diakóssia
14	dhekatéssera	300	triakóssia
15	dhekepénde	1000	khília
16	dhekaéxi	2000	dhío khiliádes
17	dhckaeftá		

TIME

Morning	to proí
Midday	to messiméri
Afternoon	to apóyevma

Evening	to vrádhi
Night	i níkhta
Yesterday	chrés
Today	simera
Tomorrow	ávrio
Early	enorís
Late	argá
When?	Póte?
Four o' clock (AM)	Stis tésseres to proí
At 5:30 PM	Stis pendémisi to apóyevma
Sunday	Kiriakí
Monday	Dheftéra
Tuesday	Tríti
Wednesday	Tetárti
Thursday	Pémpti
Friday	Paraskeví
Saturday	Sávato
Hour	óra
Day	iméra
Week	evdhomádha
Month	mínas
Year	chrónos

HOTEL

Hotel	xenodhokhío
Room	dhomátio
Bathroom	bánio
Bed	kreváti
Cover	kouvérta
Pillow	maxilári
Lamp	lámba
Cold water	krío neró
Hot water	zestó neró
Key	klidhí
Guest	xénos
Do you have a room with 2 beds?	Échete éna dhíklino dhomátio?
I am staying only one night	Tha mino mia níkhta

| Can I pay with a credit card? | Boró na pliróso me aftí ti pistotiki kárta? |
| Do you accept travelers cheques? | Pérnete travellers cheques? |

RESTAURANTS

Restaurant	estiatório
Food	fayitó
Table	trapézi
Chair	karékla
Napkin	petséta
Plate	piáto
Cup	flitzáni
Glass	potíri
Fork	piroúni
Spoon	koutáli
Knife	machéri
Waiter	garsóni
Waterboy	mikrós
Check	loghariasmós
Tip	pourboire
Menu	katáloghos
Hors d'oeuvres	orektiká
Bread	psomí
Water	neró
Wine	krassí
Beer	bíra
Milk	ghála
Meat	kréas
Fish	psária
Chicken	kotópoulo
Hot	zestós
Cold	kríos

AROUND TOWN

Street	othós
Square	platía
Boulevard	leofóros
Attention!	Prossochí!

Forbidden	Apaghorévete
Open	aniktós
Shut	klistós
Entrance	íssodhos
Exit	éxodhos
Toilet	toualéta
Women	ghynekón
Men	andhrón
Store	maghazí
Kiosk	períptero
Post office	takhidhromío
Letter	ghrámma
Stamp	grammatósimo
Airmail	aeroporikós
Telephone	tiléfono
Telegram	tilegráfima
How much does it cost?	Póso káni aftó?
Bank	trápeza
Money	khrímata
Drachmas	drachmés
I would like to exchange a cheque	Thélo na haláxo éna tsek.
Laundry	plidirio
Dry-cleaning	katharistírio
I need it tomorrow	Prépi na íne étimo ávrio to proí

ON THE ROAD

Automobile	aftokínito
Bus	leoforío
Taxi	taxi
Motorcycle	motosikléta
Bicycle	podhílato
Ship	plío **or** karávi
Airplane	aeropláno
Railroad station	stathmós trénou
Stop(bus)	stássi
Map	khártis
Ticket	issitírio

Gas station	pratírion venzinis
Gas	venzini
Oil	ládhi
Kilometer	khiliómetro
Straight ahead	kat efthían
Right	dhexiá
Left	aristerá
Opposite	apénandi
One way	aplo
Roundtrip (return)	me epistrofí
Quickly	grígora
Slowly	sighá
Where is-?	Pou íne?-
How many hours?	Pósses óres?
When does the bus leave?	Tí óra févyi to leoforío?